Contents

Less puzzle, more plan

The picture on the box shows where the jigsaw's pieces fit. The scaffolding around the growing building outlines its final shape and scale. This book attempts to be to Christian living what the picture is to the jigsaw and the scaffolding to the architect's design. It offers the Bible's perspective and framework, so that we can see how the pieces of our lives come together and then build with confidence. Less of the puzzle, more of the plan.

The chapters explore this theme and apply it to many areas of life. Each ends with an interlude (in a different typeface) to illustrate the theme in a contrasting way – a case study or biography, a comment or a quotation, poetry or testimony.

My warmest thanks go to *Alistair, Andy, Bev, Claire, Hazel, Jason, Jayne, John, Joy, Richard, Sophie, Tim*. They read the manuscript and made perceptive comments. Any failure to reach their mark is entirely mine. I am hugely in their debt – as I am to Jenny Mann, a brilliant PA who got it all into shape.

Between them they represent an age-range from students to over-sixties; mothers and fathers; singles and marrieds; teachers and dentists; police officers and systems analysts; people in both 'Christian' and 'secular' work; in the UK and other countries. A cross-section of possible readers?

Have you ever had trouble?

Chris had absolutely zero Christianity in his background. His parents never went to church and had never sent him. He could not remember coming across a Christian until he joined a new company when he was twenty-four. Two of the eight others in his division were Christians. He noticed that they did not merely go to church, but lived out their Christianity too.

He was suspicious of them at first, but ended up thinking that they were great people to be with: good fun, thoughtful, caring, definite but not pushy. After a time he found himself asking them questions. What did they believe and why? What gave them what he admitted was an attractive lifestyle? Where did they find the courage occasionally to stand out from others over some ethical issue in company policy? Why didn't they get drunk like some of the others? Most of all, he was drawn to them because their lives seemed to make sense – and he was pretty sure that his did not. He could not deny that their lives seemed to be integrated, to have a basis and a purpose. They seemed to be 'together' people.

Gradually he conceded to himself that there must be a connection between their beliefs and the poise and coherence of their lives. He began to look into their convictions and, in the end, after long reflection and many conversations, he put his trust in Jesus. It was all totally new to him. Chris into religion – he could hardly believe it, but it was real enough and he threw himself into learning the faith and working it out. He wanted and knew that he needed a framework to his life, something to hold it together.

After his conversion, his Christian friends did him proud. One met him every week in a lunch hour, to read the Bible, pray and talk. They introduced him to a fine church, which stretched his heart and mind. They fed him the occasional good Christian book and did all that they could to encourage him.

Then, with little warning to its employees, the company had to 'rationalize' by declaring some redundancies, Chris included. That in itself did not throw him too much. He had earlier learnt how God could help him cope with the death of a close relative. But he did have to uproot and go to another part of the country when he found his next job. That broke the regular network of Christian friends and church. The church he took up with was lively, but 'not the same'. Some emphases were new to him and he didn't quite know how to weigh them up. For the first time he came across disagreements between Christians, some of whom seemed to him to major on minors. He was the only Christian in his new firm and often found that hard. Some of his attempts to put in a good word for Jesus backfired. His move indirectly led to the break-up of a long-running relationship.

When he tried to discuss some of his problems with his new Christian friends, he got the impression that they felt him a little deficient. They left him feeling more condemned than encouraged. He found himself thinking that to struggle was the same as to be defeated. He began to think the unthinkable: did his Christian life add up after all? What had first drawn him into the faith (that here was truth that made sense of life) now seemed in doubt.

This book is for people, of all ages and both sexes, like Chris. His experience can happen to anyone. Have you ever had trouble making sense of your Christian life?

1

Where's the sense?

The thirteen-year-old was listening to his favourite music – with his father, on this occasion. They got on well with each other. The son was ecstatic about his music. Dad was enjoying it too and after a while he asked: 'What do you think makes it good? Why do you like it so much?' 'I just like it – it's good.' He asked again, a little later. The son thought for a while and then answered: 'I don't understand why you have to analyse everything. The trouble for your generation, Dad, was that everything had to have a meaning. Now things are different: nothing has to have a meaning any more.' A very postmodern reply.

People today don't go in for coherence, for the big picture, for trying to make sense of things. Well, some people don't, for Christians are a bit different. 'No sense, no meaning' does not satisfy our heads or our hearts. For one thing, it does not stand up very well against the person of

Christ, unless he is merely the privatized deity of our own little religious world. He is, rather, *the* Lord, as well as our Lord. He has all authority in heaven and earth. He is supreme over all creation and his lordship embraces the whole of life. If that is so, there must be some direction, some pattern to what he is about and what goes on in our lives. On this basis we feel that we should be able to get the picture. This does not mean that we will discern the whole picture here and now. As Paul wrote: 'Now we see but a poor reflection … Now I know in part'. It is only in the life to come that 'we shall see face to face' and 'shall know fully' (1 Corinthians 13:12).

It is possible, however, to see something now. We can know in part. We can discern the broad outlines of the picture, even if many features will not come fully clear until after the end of time.

The trouble is that we often have difficulty in seeing those features that God has unveiled here. Our life as Christians frequently does not seem to hang together. It feels like a collection of random bits and pieces, of things we do that are good and worthy but somehow don't have any uniting principle. We pray. We read the Bible. We go to church. We give. We work. We try to obey God. We care for the family. We take an interest in missions. These are the jigsaw pieces. But some seem the wrong shape. Others appear to be missing, or from another picture. They just don't fit and we feel they should; we want them to. These are all proper things for a Christian to do, but they don't add up to anything coherent. So where is the whole picture?

Unanswered questions

Then there is the puzzlement that comes from unanswered

questions. Sometimes we are baffled by the way our circumstances turn out. I knew a couple whose faith was seriously dented when they had a car accident. 'But we had prayed about it and trusted our journey to God,' they said. They could make no sense of the setback. They thought that something must have gone fundamentally wrong – with God – for that to happen.

They survived the collision unscathed, but sometimes much more serious events break into ordered lives. A thirty-two-year-old Christian recently developed cancer and was dead within thirty days. A friend nearly bled to death after an electric tool slipped and cut the artery in his wrist. A staff worker in a member movement within the International Fellowship of Evangelical Students lost her husband in an air crash, leaving her alone with their three young children. Another was driving with her husband and children when he was shot by terrorists before their eyes – and she was pregnant with their next child.

All the ordinary tragedies of life can happen to Christians: redundancy, ill-health, burn-out, broken relationships, failed exams, bereavement. We can half-understand those things happening to people who do not know God, but Christians have God as Father; what then is he doing? And if he has not forsaken us and is doing something, what is that something?

Silence from God

In all these circumstances we turn to prayer. We offer the situation to God and plead for his help and deliverance. We have known many answers in the past, but now – silence. Others in the home-group talk of answers to prayer this week, but for us – nothing. The crash happens, the friend dies, the boss calls us in. Why doesn't our prayer work? We are all taught that prayer changes things, that God hears and loves to answer. We take comfort from the conviction that 'Yes', 'No' and 'Wait' are all answers, but it is still tough to make sense of God and prayer while standing at a graveside or queuing in the Job Centre.

It is easy to feel that God owes us something. We pray in the belief that God will honour those who honour him (1 Samuel 2:30). We know we are nowhere near perfect, but we have tried to put God first in our friendships, family, job and church. We've tried to live Christianly in the secular world. But then we look at that other family: all their children have turned out to be shining Christians and ours show hints of rebellion. We look at a friend, who gives little time to the church while bombing along in her career, with a salary to match; and we, who give much to the church in every sense, peg along with an unjustly modest income. Where is God's 'honouring' in all that? Where is justice?

No clinching argument

It is sometimes difficult to make sense of our Christian witness. We try to live for Christ in the neighbourhood, at the office or on campus. We engineer the odd opening for a Christian comment. Maybe opportunities open up from time to time. But we never seem to be able to produce the punch-line. The clinching argument never seems to come. Our friends or colleagues seem interested, occasionally, but basically content to truck along as they are. We feel that the gospel should have some impact – after all, it is the power of God to save. What is going on? How can we be so dumb and others so deaf? Such thoughts can easily leave us feeling more guilty than motivated.

What can you expect?

Then there is the matter of expectations. 'Everything will be new when you become a Christian: new life, new joy, new power.' The promises made to us sounded so absolute, so unqualified, seeming to leave no room for any of the carry-over from our non-Christian days. Sometimes this expectation of total change was fostered by the testimonies we heard, which depicted a complete contrast between the before and the after: 'I used to live totally for myself, but then God came in and all I want now is to please him.' Nothing prepared us for any element of struggle or doubt; it was all so clear-cut. No-one told us that the Christian life was, by definition, entering into a conflict, facing possible rejection or taking up a cross.

A little later, when we had realized that as new creatures we still had some old failings, we may have come across great promises: 'If you come into this experience, if you let God work in his way, if you really seek him … then you can rise above the old ways and reach a higher plane of spiritual experience.' It seemed that we could know God's power and his heart in a new and deeper way, that we would find God's true reviving work. Those who urged these things on us seemed very authoritative and persuasive, apparently with a direct access to God that was quite out of our reach. So we went to the recommended events and felt genuinely uplifted.

Old temptations

But – there is, sooner or later, always a 'but'. Monday morning follows Saturday night and Sunday. The valley lies at the foot of the mountain. The intensity of experience does not last. Life does not deliver what the claims offered. When we're away from the crowd or the group, life – if we are honest – can be pretty down. Old temptations, we find, have not disappeared. We feel as though we could almost give a testimony at the Sunday night celebration; the atmosphere is upbeat, people are really praising God, life is great. On Monday at the office, we can't even open our mouth for God when opportunity stares us in the face.

Maybe we know we drank too much before we were converted and wonder whether we are turning back to it too easily or regularly in a time of stress at work. We know we shouldn't sneak a look at certain magazines we used to get, but are caught between not wanting to, yet still being strongly tempted. What is most apparent is the insistent question of how to make sense of all this in the light of what we know of the Christian life from the Bible.

Our assurance can also fluctuate with the rise and fall of our feelings. We know that ultimately our assurance that God accepts us depends on what he has done for us in Jesus; we know that in our heads. But our hearts tell us something else; in practice our sense of assurance is closely linked to what is happening to us and to how we feel. If we are caught up in some of the situations outlined above, we may not feel that God loves us. We may know in our heads that he loves us all the time, but it is hard to believe that when circumstances turn against us.

Sometimes, when we have questions, we cannot easily see where or how we could raise them. We hesitate to do so at church, because we might be the only ones with such questions. There is no point in unsettling the others, when they all seem so serene and untroubled. Maybe we fear upsetting the leaders; they might see questions as a threat to their position. If we then raise a question, we may be sidelined as 'not wholly committed'. Perhaps it is better to keep our peace and bottle up the questions. Life is easier if we conform, except that then we will begin to add the church to the list of things that don't make sense to us.

This in turn prompts us to wonder if we genuinely 'belong'. We know we are accepted if we basically go along with the ways of the church or group – if our dress, language and general lifestyle more or less conform. But maybe our sense of belonging comes more from the fact that we fit the mould than from being accepted for who we are. And if, in extreme cases, everyone is conforming, where are the real human beings?

Monday morning

As we move each week from Sunday to Monday, there are further problems. What is the connection between church and world, between the Bible and life, between 'worship' and work? A routine Sunday seems like a separate compartment, especially if the preacher urges us at the start to put from our minds all the affairs and business of the week and just concentrate on God. Isn't God the God of days two to seven, as well as of day one? Sunday is devoted to the spiritual and pious aspects of life, unrelated to the earthy and practical. Pulpit exhortations to serve God are often applied to the need for Sunday School teachers, not for Christian nurses or computer programmers. Prayer for the world is focused on missionaries more than on managers. The world is compartmentalized, with one area for God, the other for ... So how does the Christian life hang together? The answer may not be obvious.

Mixed-up me

Finally comes the question of how I can make sense of myself. What a bizarre mixture I am. I am not what I was, but neither am I what I should be and nowhere near what I will be. I love God, but regularly put myself first. I want holiness, but at the same time court temptation. I pray, but live as though I can depend on myself. I am deeply perplexed by the evil in my own heart and glad no-one can see it. At other times I genuinely delight in God and love his law. Who can make sense of me?

Depressed, even devastated

You and I could both list many other areas where our Christian lives seem baffling. These are serious issues. When we are confused, we can gradually become depressed and even devastated. It is tough to try to believe in something that doesn't seem to add up. The continual drip, drip of 'Why?' questions can wear away the stone of faith, especially if we have no outlet for airing those questions with those who will understand.

Whether or not people have left their faith over those issues only God knows; some have certainly drifted out of churches – and others have been tempted to, disillusioned with approaches that are simplistic, dry or authoritarian.

We can devise various methods to deal with such issues. Some Christians seem blissfully unaware of them, which is fine until a sudden unforeseen event throws up questions they have never faced before. Others are aware of questions, but try to ignore them, maybe by busying themselves in work or church or family. Others know that they are trying to suppress the questions and live uneasily as a result, half fearing to examine the basis of their faith, conforming outwardly but hesitant inwardly.

These issues cannot be ignored and will not go away. No Christian can postpone them indefinitely. God made us to think, as well as to feel and decide and relate; to think includes having questions. We are only denying our created nature if we don't allow ourselves to think. So the wise Christian faces the questions honestly and humbly takes them to God, to the Bible. When we do that, we quickly discover that we are in good company.

I once wrote a review of a little book entitled *Letters to a Devastated Christian*, by an American author, Gene Edwards (Christian Books, 1979). He basically described the feelings of any Christian who has been devastated by such factors as failed expectations, authoritarian leadership or teaching, not being allowed to raise questions or in other ways feeling let down by God, circumstances or other Christians – in other words, Christians who despaired of making sense of their church experience or their Christian lives. The mere fact of the review drawing attention to the book prompted a response that was absolutely overwhelming from Christians who identified with Edwards. Letters poured in, far outnumbering those I had received on any other topic. There were obviously a lot of devastated Christians out there.

More importantly, the Bible is characteristically honest in showing us people who also had trouble making sense of life. We are not told explicitly whether Abraham had a 'Why?' question or two about offering his only son (Genesis 22), but we suspect that, in the same situation, we would have. David knew what it was to be cast down in his soul, disturbed in his inner being. He went around mourning, oppressed by his enemy. He faced people taunting him with 'Where is your God?' He remembered what he used to experience – joy and thanksgiving with all the other worshippers – but now he felt God had forgotten him. He was up against ungodly, deceitful and wicked men (Psalms 42 – 43). What on earth was God doing?

In another psalm Asaph confessed that his faith was wobbling, nearly losing its foothold, because 'I envied the arrogant when I saw the prosperity of the wicked'. He thought that he had kept his heart pure for nothing, that he had tried to live an upright life, but had not been rewarded; rather, the ungodly had prospered. How could he make sense of that? Shouldn't good triumph and evil be punished? The moral order in which he believed, and to which he thought God was pledged, seemed to be stood on its head (Psalm 73).

And then there is the writer of Ecclesiastes, suggesting rather cogently that life can seem to have a total futility to it: ' "Meaningless! Meaningless!" says the Teacher. "Utterly meaningless! Everything is meaningless!" ' (Ecclesiastes 1:2).

Paul wrestled

Paul certainly wrestled with the problem of how to understand himself. There is some debate as to whether Paul is speaking of life after conversion when he writes: 'I do not understand what I do. For what I want to do I do not do, but what I hate I do … I have the desire to do what is good, but I cannot carry it out. For what I do is not the good I want to do …' (Romans 7:15–19). Such expressions certainly tally with the experience of some believers.

The martyrs' question

The last book of the Bible even pictures Christian martyrs who have reached heaven, but who still have a question on their minds: 'the souls of those who had been slain because of the word of God ... called out in a loud voice, "How long, Sovereign Lord, holy and true, until you judge the inhabitants of the earth and avenge our blood?"' (Revelation 6:9–10). They were trying to make sense of why judgment had not already come; if God is holy and true, surely he cannot tolerate evil for a moment?

The most poignant 'Why?'

Undoubtedly the most poignant 'Why?' question of all time came from the lips of Jesus on the cross. Even though he knew that he had come to earth specifically for 'this hour', even though he knew his Father's will about the cross and was entirely at one with it (John 12:27), he still cried out in a loud voice: 'My God, my God, why have you forsaken me?' (Matthew 27:46). The ultimate mystery: the Father forsaking the Son. While the Bible unpacks the reasons for this, the point here is that Jesus was so moved, sad and troubled that he felt his soul overwhelmed with sorrow to the point of death (Matthew 26:37–38). This was the ultimate 'Why?' question. Was there no other way? Did it have to be the cross?

We are not the first to struggle at times with how to make sense of our lives.

Unhappy pursuit

Long on promise, short on delivery: that is how many feel about society. The motor industry advertisers are certainly not afraid to promise. 'You can be sure' of our brand of petrol; 'If only every car were as reliable' as our make. The cynics behind one blockbuster advertisement virtually promised that when you pick up the keys of your new car, 'You'll find the key to your life.'

A perfume manufacturer says that, while his laboratories produce perfume, his shops sell dreams. The beauty aids, the slimming products, the fashion magazines, for women and men, all offer promises to help us in the central purposes of life: to become confident and to pursue happiness. And because all that depends on our image; our looks, our clothes, our car, our salary ... we are ripe for all that the advertisers offer us. In the process we endlessly compare ourselves with others. This is why, in the TV advertising world, magic dressed up as reality is rife.

The result? Large amounts of misery. As Walter Lippman (the American columnist) said, the pursuit of happiness is a most unhappy pursuit. Christians are not immune to those influences either.

Clinical psychologist Oliver James, writing about 'the angst of normal people like us', notes that a woman in her mid-twenties today is between three and ten times more likely to be depressed than her grandmother was at the same age. He adds:

Few of us are free from the unending conflict between living healthy lives and the short-term gratification of drugs of solace (including food as well as tobacco, alcohol and illegal drugs) ... Many of us

21

feel permanently run down, below par emotionally, highly irritable ... and we seek these temporary reliefs (*Britain on the Couch* [Century, 1997]).

He describes the resultant 'epidemic of anxious attachment' and 'the huge expectation now placed on relationships as an almost religious salvation' – an expectation undermined by 'the likelihood of those relationships being broken and disrupted'.

Other commentators have made similar observations of a society frantically searching for happiness. So what is the way out? How can society find confidence and happiness? Many people's solution (like Oliver James's) is to take Prozac. That may calm us down or raise our levels of serotonin (the so-called 'happiness chemical'), but it won't put meaning into anyone's life.

How can people make sense of life on that basis? No wonder a sad seventy-three-year-old said recently: 'When you're dead, you're dead. That's the meaning of life.' No wonder our generation is so much more likely to be miserable than our grandparents. Take God away and what sense is left?

Ours is not the first generation to need reminding that 'life under the sun', life in a fallen world that pushes God out, 'is meaningless'. We have only to read the book of Ecclesiastes. Nothing is new under the sun and the Bible reminds us of the truth of that statement.

As Christians we may sometimes have trouble making sense of life, but we live in the knowledge that God *is*. God exists and so meaning exists. Moreover, we have open access to his presence, through his Son's death in our place; and to his mind, as his Book unfolds to us the sense behind the circumstances.

2
Wrong expectations

Sometimes, when life does not make sense, the reasons are obvious. If we are out of step with God, if we know that we are going against his will, if we are neglecting our Maker's instructions in any area, then we will clearly be out of line with the meaning God wants our lives to have. The prodigal son came to a right mind only after he had wasted all his money on frivolous living; his selfish lifestyle had made 'non-sense' of his life. Disobedience or plain self-centredness will not help us to put the pieces of life together.

We can see the effects of disobedience in this area. But why does life not fall into place when we are seeking to be obedient to God? We all know that, even if we are walking with God, we may still feel mystified at the way our life is going. We have seen some of the typical situations that make us feel that way. So why do we have these recurring struggles that can take such a mental and emotional toll?

One of the basic reasons is that we may mistake what the Bible teaches about God, life and what we may expect from him.

The gap

Take the gap that we sense between Sunday and Monday, the world of church and the world of work. How do they relate? Are they connected or separate? There is an impression in some Christian circles that one is the spiritual sphere, the other the secular or worldly sphere. We can get the idea that what goes on in one (prayer, praise, preaching, gospel) is to do with the central purpose of life; and that what goes on in the other (work, salaries, production, sales) is subsidiary, a necessary evil, a means to an end. We sense God in the one, we merely exist in the other.

If we are affected by that view, life at work will not make much sense. After all, what is its ultimate point? Merely by being there, incipient materialism is probably creeping up on us. We feel like second-class citizens, since many churches pray regularly for their missionaries, but rarely for their managers or midwives. The 'non-sense' factor increases if we mistake what the Bible teaches about work, a topic we look at in chapter 14.

That same mistake lay behind my friends' perplexity over their car crash. Their problem was that what happened did not fit into their idea of God. They expected more than he had promised in the Bible. On their view, he should never have allowed the accident, given that they had prayed about it. Reality was one thing, their idea of God another. God did not do what he ought to do, so no wonder their life puzzled them. They had accepted a view of God that did not reflect the Bible's.

Promising too much

Or think of some of the teachings that offer in God's name more than he has actually promised: 'If you let yourself go and surrender to God, you will know his supernatural power ...' We seek to follow the exhortation and it all begins to work out. We sense that life has become different, that we have moved a stage on and up. But, gradually or suddenly, we begin to bump up against some of our old temptations. Some old failings return, along with a growing awareness that we cannot live on cloud nine and are a long way from heaven. It feels as though 'normal service has been resumed'.

Why? The problem is the tension between the desires or expectations on the one hand, and the realities of life and ourselves on the other. The promise was of something akin to heaven now. The reality tells us that we are redeemed, but still definitely on earth. No wonder we find life a bit mystifying.

Wrong expectations

The realities of life are set out in the Bible; they do not match all the things that 'could be' according to some. What we expect to happen (on the basis of the extravagant promises some make, for example) may not happen. That couple in the previous chapter expected God to preserve them from an accident; then the crash came. The false promise offered life on a spiritual plane; our experience bumped up against reality and told us we were still on earth.

The 'can't see where it's heading' feeling comes from teaching that does not reflect what God's Word says about the way things are now in God's world. Wrong teaching leads to wrong understanding; the resulting clash with reality leads us into deflating experiences. It is we who create unreal worlds if we opt for human wisdom rather than the Bible's.

Something we lack

Sometimes claims or terminology can give the impression that others have something that we lack; and, in response, we may feel substandard. It may well be that there is something we need or can learn, for we all have a long way to go. But it may also be that they are using biblical words or concepts in an unbiblical way, or merely deceiving themselves.

In the Bible God never promises an accident-free life. He never promises an instant cure for all our feelings and weaknesses. He never divides life up into spiritual and secular compartments. He never says that witnessing will be easy or that there is a formula for success. He never offers the prospect of sinless perfection or total power in this life or an end to inner struggles. We need to adjust our thinking to the Bible, to God; we are on a fool's errand if we try to press God into our world or make him fit into our box.

Give me patience!

Take an everyday example: we may work with irritating, fractious, pernickety colleagues who test our patience to the limit. 'I can do everything through Christ who strengthens me', quotes a pious friend. 'Just ask and trust God. He will give you patience.' 'Give me patience', we plead to God. What happens? Nothing very dramatic. 'If only you'd give me patience, Lord. Why don't you help me? Where's the purpose in all this?'

God, we learn, does not give patience in a neat complete package, but teaches us patience through experience. Our patience goes on being tested every single day – it feels like every single moment. There is no divine parachute-drop to deliver 'patience'. God tells us, 'train yourself to be godly' (1 Timothy 4:7), to put in the effort and discipline, which means that his answer is by way of a long-term regime for spiritual fitness and patience, not a quick-fix solution.

Proper goals

It is the same in other areas of our Christian life. We want and need holiness, power, love, faith, grace, endurance. We want to be rid of sin and failure. All these are proper goals for the Christian, but we must seek them in God's way. God does not offer one all-transforming experience, but an ongoing life of trusting and obeying, a pilgrim marathon that sometimes has more hard slog than heavenly sunshine.

That prospect is not 100% appealing, which is one reason why so many instant solutions are offered. 'Go to these meetings ... have this experience ... reach out and touch ... let yourself go ... and you will be overwhelmed, uplifted ... Your days as a plodding Christian will be over.'

This is not the Christian life offered in the Bible, but a human construct – very plausible and 'spiritual', but a human construct nonetheless and therefore a letdown in the end. This does not mean, of course, that God never gives unusual or remarkable experiences of himself to his people, as he did in Bible times. It simply means that we must not rely on such experiences to solve all our particular problems. God is a Father, not a servant at our beck and call.

Buy now, pay later

Society today lives on instant gratification. Flick to the next channel if this one does not grab us. Let the bank take the waiting out of wanting. Turn to another relationship when the present one begins to bore.

Church culture echoes too much of this. The immediate demand and promise of much teaching is way off God's line in the Bible. Take the honours list of great men and women of faith in Hebrews 11. 'These were all commended for their faith, yet none of them received what had been promised' (Hebrews 11:39). None. They had the kind of faith we should emulate, yet none received even delayed gratification in their earthly life. This is why the writer tells us that we need to run the Christian race with patience or perseverance (Hebrews 12:1), so that (without instant gratification) we do not grow weary or lose heart. They made sense of life, for all their troubles; the rest of this book will show how sticking close to what God has said can do the same for us, so that the pieces of life fit together.

Where the power lies

A student was invited in Freshers' Week to join a 'Just Looking' group. When people began to get out their copies of a gospel, he left immediately. He didn't want to be studying that. Later he was given a copy as part of a gospel distribution, but did not read it until the summer term. As he started to read it, he became gripped. In fact, he was so intrigued that he read the entire New Testament. Then he decided that, to understand the New Testament, he needed to read the Old. So he did, over the course of the summer. All the while, God was speaking to him, persuading him of his existence, reality and truth.

When he returned the following October, again he met a Christian who invited him to another 'Just Looking' group. The friendship grew and this time he stayed. His reading had led him to faith in Christ. The Bible had come to make such sense that he could no longer resist it.

It can be difficult to trace when or where the Holy Spirit is working. For a whole year nothing seemed to be happening in that student. Jesus himself sounded a note of caution about this: 'The wind blows. ... You hear its sound, but you cannot tell where it comes from or where it is going. So it is with everyone born of the Spirit' (John 3:8).

It is perhaps easier to trace *how* the Spirit works, because God has said a lot about that in the Bible. Paul affirmed that 'the gospel ... is the power of God for the salvation of everyone who believes' (Romans 1:16). The message is the power, he says: the plain, straightforward message, in appropriate words – *that* is the power of God to save guilty people.

This is why Jesus told people to change the direction of their lives and believe his message (Mark 1:15). And why he said: 'You will know the truth, and the truth will set you free' (John 8:32).

This is the way the Spirit of truth works: he convicts the world of its guilt and God's solution (John 16:8–13).

29

He gave the message, put it down in writing and constantly keeps it alive. He opens hearts to 'respond to [the] message' (Acts 16:14). He works in people so that 'faith comes from hearing the message … the word of Christ' (Romans 10:17). The result of the Spirit working in this way is that new Christians from the start have a firm foundation for their faith – the objective Word of God.

This does not mean that there is some neat 'gospel formula' that will magically turn people to Christ. People can be converted just by reading the gospel of Luke or John. But many will have questions that need to be answered, misunderstandings that need to be cleared up. Many will never come near the Lord without prayer and friendship. This is why Paul urged his readers to pray that 'words may be given me so that I will fearlessly make known … the gospel' (Ephesians 6:19). This is also why Jesus was so totally into friendship. It was out of friendship that he spoke his words to ordinary people (Luke 15).

Christian lifestyle, crucial as it is, is not enough. It is the message that is the power. The Spirit had John's gospel written so that we may read and believe (John 20:31). God has made it powerful in itself.

3
Back to the source

Secular views can never make sense of life, for they leave out of account the ultimate reality, God. This is what lies behind the Bible's repeated assertion that 'The fear of the LORD is the beginning of wisdom' (Psalm 111:10), the beginning of making sense. If we are to find coherence in life, God must speak. And he has. He has not left us to guess his thinking, but has given us the Bible precisely to lead us through life.

It does not tell us everything we may want to know, but it does give us everything we need for living and becoming godly (2 Peter 1:3). This is sufficient for us to begin to put the pieces of life together and gradually see more and more of his overall picture. That picture does not come into focus all at once and we should not expect it to do so, though we can expect to grasp more as we go through life with God. As we start the Christian life, the central character and action come into focus. As we move on more and more becomes clear. Finally, when we reach glory, every detail will stand out in sharp relief. That final vision will make sense of everything, and will take our breath away.

Conversely, the further we are from God, the further we are from sense. The closer we are to his mind, the closer we are to understanding what is going on. This is why sticking close to the Bible is our only adequate help in trying to make sense of life and to know how to live. So how does the Bible help us? The beauty of it is that it exactly matches and describes what is, what we find in life. When we get into it seriously, and not just to look for helpful random verses, it helps us in many ways.

Matching our experience

First, it ties in with our experience. Whatever we may experience we will find described in the Bible's pages. The Bible takes account of all that can happen to us. Elation, depression; joy, sorrow; victory, defeat; understanding, bafflement; encouragement, let-downs; fidelity, betrayal; riches, poverty; friendships, loneliness; loving, hating; assurance, uncertainty; expectations, disappointments; well-being, suffering; hope, fear; living, dying. All the experiences of life today are there in the Guide. No aspect of our experience is outside the Bible's scope. This is because God, whose Spirit caused the Bible to be written, knows us through and through. He shows this in the Bible's accounts of individuals or groups. The narrative books of the Bible are alive with meaning. They describe people of identical feelings and temptations to us. We are there, in those pages. 'No temptation has seized you except what is common among people' (1 Corinthians 10:13). 'Elijah was human just as we are' (James 5:17).

The match between the Bible and our experience is a great source of assurance and understanding. If we get hold of what the Bible says and discard mistaken views, we will find that life begins to make sense. It is not that the Bible will yield a specific or immediate explanation of that car crash or your redundancy. God did not give Joseph an immediate explanation of why his brothers threw him into a cistern or sold him as a slave into Egypt. It was only years later that Joseph came to full understanding and could say to his brothers: 'You intended to harm me, but God intended it for good to accomplish ... the saving of many lives' (Genesis 50:20).

Providing a framework

Second, the Bible gives us a framework for our understanding. We will see more of what this is as the story unfolds, but essentially God gives us his picture of life here and hereafter, his set of clues as to what is going on. All that enables us by his Spirit to make sense of the kinds of experiences we have, even if we sometimes have to wait to see how a particular experience fits with the overall plan.

The Bible tells us what we can expect from God, from the devil, from ourselves, from life. It gives us the true view of every aspect of life: of prayer, of self-understanding, of God's present and ultimate purposes. Supremely, it gives us the true knowledge of God, so that our hopes are surely, not falsely, based.

Offering a prescription

Third, and perhaps most important of all, the Bible is God's living voice to guide us today. God speaks to us precisely where we are, whatever our state or present experience. He does not wait until we have reached a certain spiritual level. With God's diagnosis comes his prescription. A friend said: 'I'm not much use to God now, but I think I will be when I'm a better Christian.' But we don't have to wait. The Bible doesn't kick in when we reach a certain level; it helps us where we are.

The Bible contains much history, but is not just about the past. It is God's record, but it is also his current testimony. It is not just what God once spoke; it is God speaking today. He is alive. Because he is eternal and does not change, what he said is what he is still saying. His 'then' word is his 'now' word. This is why the Bible should be so central to the church and our individual lives.

This is not always clear. The next time you are in a church or a Christian Union meeting, ask yourself: 'Where are they getting what they say in God's name? What is the source of their message? What really makes them come alive? What moves them?'

Perhaps it is the bee in the preacher's bonnet. It may *sound* biblical, but actually takes little notice of any passage. Perhaps the sharing time in a home-group squeezes the Bible out as people are absorbed in each other's situations. It could be a claim to a prophecy, as though God himself is speaking: 'My dear children, I say to you ...' It could be someone with a picture: 'God wants me to bring this to you ...'

If people get their buzz from sources other than the Bible, we are on the way to losing God's plot. If such items take centre stage, they relegate the Bible from its proper place. No-one announces that this is what is happening; no-one may want it to happen; the Bible may be opened, but then misused or passed over. In extreme cases it may not even be opened at all. We all acknowledge that we should honour the Bible. But if in the event we listen more to our bees, tradition, words or experiences – even if we persuade ourselves that they are from God – then we are actually saying that we can listen elsewhere to hear God today.

'Experiences that chime in with the present culture may be good, or they may not. The Bible, however, as the Holy Spirit's chosen method of guiding the church throughout time, has outlived a thousand generations of different experiences and influences', as Oliver Barclay points out in *Evangelicalism in Britain 1935–1995* (IVP, 1997).

Now and then

Sometimes it has been said that the Bible is God's 'then' word, whereas our current need is for his 'now' word. We want to be obeying God today, not locked into a tradition, however worthy. And since the Bible is from the past, it needs to be updated by new or 'now' words from God. We then take these words and test them by Scripture to see if they match up. The Bible becomes more of a testbook for occasional reference than a textbook for constant use.

Yet the Bible tells us to 'test everything' (1 Thessalonians 5:21) and 'weigh carefully' anything that is said by way of prophecy (1 Corinthians 14:29). The Bible must be used in any such checking-out exercise. More fundamentally, we are to turn to it regularly and continuously all through our life. If we use it only to test some other word, we will be neglecting its prime purpose as God's source of wisdom and belittling the authority of God himself.

Any good textbook must be up to date and comprehensive, providing all the information we need. The Bible claims to be sufficient to equip the Christian for every good work (2 Timothy 3:16). It needs to be prayerfully and thoughtfully applied, but it never needs to be supplemented by fresh words – as though it were not always up to date. It is the fount and source of all the truth of God. We will be moving away from truly loving God if ever we drift away from the sufficiency of his Word.

Sometimes the 'now' approach to the Bible goes in tandem with disparaging the past. What God is doing today is what counts. History is history. God is always doing new things and we dare not live in the past. The intent of such thinking is to be engaging with today and serving God in our generation. Strictly speaking, however, it is a slur on God. He is the God of all ages, the same yesterday, today and for ever. If 'God is doing a new thing in our generation', why has he deprived Christians of it for twenty centuries? What kind of a God does that make him? Are we holier or more deserving?

What are past moments to us are always present moments to God. He is to be honoured for all he has done in every period. How can we thank him if we do not stop to remember? How can we avoid repeating past mistakes if we do not listen to the past? Of course, God is also at work now, but his present work is always consistent with what he has already done. God does not make U-turns.

We, however, may be at a crossroads in these matters, according to Oliver Barclay:

There are two main streams emerging in the evangelical community, and this division may prove more fundamental in its long-term effects than any other. It runs right across denominational distinctives, charismatic and non-charismatic divisions and any

36

special-interest and party groupings. It is between those who make the Bible effectively, and not only theoretically, the mainstay of their ministry, and those who do not. (The former) will ... produce strong Christians who are able to grapple with all kinds of issues in life, and to face the really tough experiences when they come. Those who fail to use the Bible in this way are almost certain to produce vulnerable Christians or painfully dependent people.

When it hits us

If we listen to the Bible regularly and prayerfully, it will consistently nourish and feed us. And we will find from time to time that the Bible also 'hits us'. It shows us some truth we had not seen before, it gives us unexpected encouragement or a painful rebuke. That is God speaking to us about our faith, our lifestyle, our obedience, our understanding. The Bible is alive and well.

Clearly, God can also show his mind on the many practical matters which the Bible does not mention: whether or not we should move house, how we should arrange our giving, which church we should join, and so on. He can give prophecy in the sense of 1 Corinthians 14:3, speaking to others 'for their strengthening, encouragement and comfort'. He can help us to know about how his mind in Scripture may be applied in particular situations, for example, about what holiness and patience will mean for a nurse in a busy ward.

Such 'speaking' always needs to be weighed (1 Corinthians 14:29). If it is truly from God, it will rest on and endorse God's revelation in the Bible. It will not be additional truth (though it may come fresh to a particular hearer), since Scripture contains all the truth that we need and that God has chosen to disclose this side of glory. In any case, if we are genuinely to strengthen, encourage and comfort, it must essentially be by what God has done and is saying; in other words, by Scripture (Romans 15:4–5). Any other comfort is essentially human.

All this is quite different from giving credence to words that effectively oust Scripture. It is almost impossible to overstate the folly and danger of that. This is why Paul and Jesus were so specific. Listen to them:

Paul committed the Ephesians 'to God and to the word of his grace, which can build you up' (Acts 20:32). He could have committed them to 'getting words from God'; he didn't. He said: 'All Scripture is God-breathed and is useful for teaching, rebuking, correcting and training in righteousness, so that God's servant may be thoroughly equipped for every good work' (2 Timothy 3:16–17). It *is* God-breathed and useful, not just *was*. Jesus said: 'You will know the truth, and the truth will set you free' (John 8:32).

Always alive and current

Now God is eternal, the God of the living and of every present moment of time. God is the contemporary of every age. He gave his Word, the Bible, in particular periods and places, but what he said is not restricted by them. His Word is always alive and current. Nothing is more up to date or modern, more culturally relevant or fitted for today than the words of the eternal God, preserved by his Spirit in the Bible. We know this in experience too, from the last time some Bible truth struck us, revealing some light on Jesus that was new to us, some fresh conviction of sin, some new ray of hope, some appropriate word. It was from the old book, that could have been gathering dust; but it was alive to us as God's Spirit went about his regular work.

The great purpose of the Bible is to turn us from our preferences to God's perspective. It stops us making our own cocktail of beliefs and gives us the pure water of God's truth. I would much prefer to believe, for example, that everyone will be saved and that all religions lead to the same God; then I could be happy about my friends and no-one would take me for a religious bigot. But the Bible does not let me think that way. I do not like the idea of judgment and eternal punishment, any more than I welcome the place of suffering. I do not like the idea of holiness; it is inhibiting and cramps my style.

The old me does not like a lot of what it finds in the Bible, and the new me in Christ still wrestles with these likes and dislikes of mine (we will see some more of them in Chapter 5 on avoiding false starts). True beliefs, however, are not settled by what we like, but by what happens to be true, by what God has disclosed in the Bible. This is its immense value. Put another way, it frees us from our own bias and blindness and opens our eyes to God's angle on everything. This is the true liberation of the imagination that many seek from their own belief-system. All this is an incalculable gift and freedom. It sets us on the way to a God-centred life, to a life that then begins to make sense.

Does God still speak today? The answer is both 'No' and 'Yes'. It is 'No' in that he does not reveal fresh truths today; all the truths we need to know are there in the Bible. He has spoken sufficiently for the whole of this life. There is a 'once-for-all' quality to the Bible that leaves no place for any additional revelation. So, if we want to hear God speak today, let us read the Bible, indeed, read it out loud. That is God's current voice; and the Spirit's basic work here is to go on making that word alive in our minds and hearts, giving us fresh insights. He was given to lead us into all truth, not by adding to the Bible, but by taking us deeper into it. As Paul wrote to Timothy: 'Reflect on what I am saying, for the Lord will give you insight ...' (2 Timothy 2:7). The Spirit does not give 'words' to substitute for searching his Word.

Does God still speak today? The answer is 'Yes' in the sense that we have a two-way conversation with God all through life. God answers prayer; that is his part of this conversation. The Spirit testifies in our hearts that we are God's children (Romans 8:15–17). At times we have a sense that we should do this or that: visit someone in hospital, write a letter, volunteer for some service, and so on.

The more we get to know God in and through the Bible, the more we will get to know his voice, especially in knowing how to apply in our lives what he says in his Word. Moreover, we will hear him increasingly in his Word. It will be no 'dead letter' but a living word, as God brings to life the revelation he gave over so many centuries with such care.

In Peter's second letter God has given us a cameo of how he wants us to live. The letter's basic *message* is about the coming 'Day of the Lord' and the close of his age. Its *method* is equally significant, with two straightforward stages: first, understand; second, respond. We will look at the response stage later; note now where Peter begins: 'First of all, you must understand' (2 Peter 3:3).

Knowledge, truth, the word, thinking ... these are his concerns. It is through their knowledge of God that they have all they need for life and godliness (2 Peter 1:3). Peter reminded them of the truth in which they had been established (1:12). He distinguished the truth from cleverly invented stories (1:16), pointing out that they had a more certain word in Scripture (1:19–21). He wanted them on their guard against error (3:17) and stimulated to wholesome thinking (3:1). So first, he says, let me inform and clarify your minds, then you will be able to respond appropriately.

The Christian life is always more than knowledge or understanding. It is never merely cerebral. It is more than trying to make sense of life or to see the big picture. *But it is never less.* The 'more' in the Christian life depends on understanding and springs out of the truth. The 'more' of joy and victory, faith and perseverance, experience and growth, witness and holiness is built on the foundation of truth. Unconcern about understanding leads to less of a Christian life, not more.

Letting the Bible make sense of our Christian lives, therefore, is indispensable for what God means us to experience. It is the entry ticket, the foundation, the springboard, the launch pad of all that can follow. And when his light dawns in our minds, his joy rises in our hearts.

The hallmark

Joy is the Christian's hallmark. David told us to seek it and practise it: 'Delight yourself in the LORD' (Psalm 37:4). Jesus (on the basis of obeying his commands and remaining in his love) wanted his joy to be in us and our joy to be complete (John 15:11). Paul wrote about 'the joy given by the Holy Spirit' (1 Thessalonians 1:6) and encouraged us to 'rejoice in the Lord always' (Philippians 4:4). Peter said that, 'even though you do not see [Christ] now, you believe in him and are filled with an inexpressible and glorious joy' (1 Peter 1:8).

Joy. What is it? Where does it come from? The Christian's joy is unique. It is essentially 'in the Lord', in God's person and character. This means it is not dependent on circumstances working out well, whether health or money or relationships or whatever else may come to us. It comes from knowing God and what he has done to bring us to himself and prepare us for glory.

Joy springs from knowing that our past is forgiven, our present is in God's hands and our future with him is assured. It rests on knowing that the big issues of life and eternity are settled.

Joy in God can remain when the going is tough, as it did for Christ, when he 'for the joy set before him endured the cross' (Hebrews 12:2). It can keep going through and despite all the trials of life and death (Romans 8:35–39). 'In all our troubles my joy knows no bounds' (2 Corinthians 7:4).

This is why making sense of the Christian life is so crucial. We can live in this joy only if we have the right and ultimate perspective. With that we can see our trials in proportion and measure them against our salvation and our hope.

Joy is not a matter of temperament or particular experiences or circumstances, but is in the Lord, who is the one constant in all the fluctuations of life. We may not always find it possible to be happy; but we can always find reason for joy in God.

So we should unashamedly enjoy our joy in the Lord. The more we know and walk with him, and the more we grasp what Jesus achieved on the cross, the more pervasive and profound will our joy become.

4
The crux of the matter

We will make sense of the Christian life only if we understand where it starts, where it ends and what its basis is. It starts with and rests on the good news Jesus brought – the gospel.

If we are uncertain or confused about what the gospel actually is, we will be confused all down the line. It is therefore worth getting our minds clear about this. In fact, every religion or philosophy, whether primitive or sophisticated, has its own 'gospel'; and every such message has its answers to four basic questions:

1. *Is anyone there?* A view of God or of ultimate reality.
2. *What's the problem?* A view of the human condition – what is right or wrong with people, what their basic need actually is.
3. *What's the answer?* A view of the solution – the remedy to whatever the problem is thought to be in 2.

4. *What's the outcome?* A view of the results – what sort of people, attitudes and actions this message produces.

What then is the Christian gospel? 'The beginning of the gospel about Jesus Christ, the Son of God … Jesus went into Galilee, proclaiming the good news of God. "The time has come," he said. "The kingdom [that is, rule or kingship] of God is near. Repent and believe the good news!" ' (Mark 1:1, 14–15). Jesus was the gospel; Jesus came with the gospel. We need to begin here if we are to make sense of our Christian life.

Jesus' message tackles the same four elements as all 'gospels', but is absolutely distinctive.

The message of Jesus

First, his view of God. Jesus shows us the kind of God we face. Two truths appear in his opening words as given by Mark. One is that God is the King, with our lives in his royal control and answerable to him. The other is that God is holy, which is why people need to turn 180 degrees round from the way that their self-centredness and rebellion are taking them. This is a sobering, humbling view of God and of our relationship to him as the holy King.

Second, his view of humanity. What kind of world do we live in? One in which people have gone wrong and are offending God. They do not need merely a little help or advice or improvement. They need to confess their guilt and turn away from their sin. As Jesus said later: 'Unless you repent, you too will all perish' (Luke 13:3, 5). If people fail to repent, they will not have some slightly less happy eternity; they will perish, be lost, be condemned.

This is a sobering, humbling view of the human condition.

Third, his view of the solution. Is there a way out for us? The dilemma lies between God's regal holiness and our human sin. The solution is the good news of Jesus coming as Saviour. That is not opened up until later in Mark and the other gospels, but then it becomes crystal clear: 'The Son of Man [came] to give his life as a ransom for many' (Mark 10:45).

Jesus came to rescue us from perishing by perishing himself as he gave his sinless life to set us free. A sobering, humbling solution.

Fourth, his view of the outcome. Where will we finish up? We will either perish, if we do not repent and believe; or we experience the good news in a transformed life of 'Come, follow me' (Mark 1:17). That means lifelong discipleship in the light of a secure eternity. A terrible outcome for those who will not repent and trust. An enthralling and uplifting outcome for those who will.

Inseparable elements

The four elements are inseparable; they are intimately and logically connected. If we start with Jesus' view of God, then that leads straight to his view of the human condition. If that is what we are like, then only his solution can deal with our dilemma. And if the cross is his solution, it will lead to gratitude and obedience. It is the same the other way round, if we start with the outcome. If the world needs Christians who will give their lives sacrificially to God, who are awed by his majesty and his mercies, whose first desire is to love and obey God, then that outcome can come only from *his* remedy to *this* condition before *this* God. All the elements hang together; there is a coherence about the gospel that satisfies our minds and makes sense of our experience.

The message of Paul

Paul presented the same four aspects. First, he opened up his view of God, the God who had promised the gospel centuries before through the prophets (Romans 1:2). This gospel reveals God's righteousness (Romans 1:17), which leads Paul to write: 'The wrath of God is being revealed from heaven ...' (Romans 1:18). That was where his gospel began, not with God's love or power, but with his wrath. The wrath of the Creator, who has scattered enough evidence about himself through his world 'that people are without excuse' (Romans 1:20).

God is revealed as a moral being, 'against all the ungodliness and wickedness' of people who 'suppress the truth by their wickedness' (Romans 1:18). From what he created he can be known in his eternal power and divine nature, but people do not want to know and he holds them accountable. This is one factor that gives life significance: the fact that there will be a judgment that takes every action or word into account means that everything we do has significance for eternity. If there were no judgment, nothing would have ultimate significance. A Hitler or a Stalin could strut the world's stage and pass on unquestioned, unaccused, their wrongs never brought to the bar of justice. God is there as Creator, for us to submit to him; and as holy, for us to obey.

Second, Paul explained what was at the root of our problem. We have suppressed the truth available to us. We exchanged the truth of God for a lie. All have sinned and fall short of the glory of God. There is no-one righteous, not even one. No-one understands or seeks God (Romans 1:18, 25; 3:23, 10). At the heart of this world, God's world, the fundamental question is moral: about righteousness and wickedness, about our guilt before a holy God. Our problem is not essentially that we feel alienated or powerless; our problem is of our own making; sin leading to guilt leading to condemnation. This is Paul's view of the human condition.

The way out

Third, Paul came to his view of the remedy: this is not a problem that 'love' can solve, because love cannot wish away the fact of human sin. The love of God cannot override or abolish the justice of God or God ceases to be God. It is not a dilemma that 'power' can solve, since it is a matter affecting God's holy character. Power cannot turn justice aside. Forgiveness needs a basis – something more than an expression of love or a demonstration of power. Forgiveness needs to have an adequate answer to the fact that we are under wrath and condemnation. We will be silent on the judgment day, with nothing at all to say in our own defence (Romans 3:19).

The only solution that could be effective (in other words, that could remove our guilt) must be one that faces and deals both with our rebellion and with God's righteousness. This is how God acted in his Son. This is where 'substitution' comes in. God 'presented [his own Son] as a sacrifice of atonement'; he, in shedding his blood, accepted the punishment for human sin (Romans 3:25). Christ was sinless, with no sin of his own to atone for; he alone, the Person of infinite goodness and worth, could bear our sin and lift God's just wrath from us.

Christ willingly came to give his life as a ransom. The Father and the Son were totally at one in conceiving and completing this sacrifice; indeed, this was a work in which all three persons of the Trinity were totally at one, since it was 'through the eternal Spirit [that Christ] offered himself' (Hebrews 9:14).

At one stroke, on that one cross, two things happened. One, God demonstrated his justice (Romans 3:25–26). He showed the world that sin mattered and that he was not sweeping it under the carpet; that righteousness was upheld; that evil did not escape its due penalty. Two, he accepted those who put their faith in Jesus (Romans 3:26). He could not justly accept them without that sacrifice. But, with that sacrifice made, the guilt of believers' sins was removed and God could be perfectly consistent with his righteous character *and* fully welcoming to those who trusted him for forgiveness. He showed himself to be wholly just and at the same time, through Christ's redeeming death, to be the one who justifies those who trust in Jesus (Romans 3:24, 26).

But for Christ and his death God would not be to us what he is. But he now gives us access because that death took place. Only this solution faces the realities of God's character and our need. Only this faces and delivers us from judgment.

Unshakeable basis

Fourth, the outcome: this gospel leads to people who have an unshakeable basis for assurance and a clear desire to give their whole lives to God. They know that no-one can now bring any charge against them, that no-one can condemn them or remove them from God's love (Romans 8:33–34). They have been acquitted by God on the basis of Christ's work (Romans 8:1–2). Moreover, they are so overwhelmed by God's mercy in Christ that they give their lives over to him as their lifelong reasonable act of service (Romans 12:1–2). They see that that is the only course that makes sense. This gospel produces believers who fear God and fear no-one else.

They no longer live for 'Number One', but for Jesus, who shed his blood for them. On this basis they have the conviction not to conform any longer to society around them. They want to be continually transformed as he renews their minds. What they want is to do the good, pleasing and perfect will of God (Romans 12:1–2).

The result of all this is that they know their identity. Identity is a vexed issue for many today, who are not sure who they are or how to find out. Believers know that they are not what they do, or drive, or own, or wear, or know; they have put aside the factors on which so many try to shape their identity and image. They are children of God.

Whereas once they had no answer to God's just accusations against them, now they have Christ's righteousness set to their account. Once guilty, they are now acquitted. Once in the condemned cell, now they are welcome before the throne of God. They are in Christ and all this is the outcome of his death in their place. This is who they are, now and for ever. And all this springs from his gospel, the message that brings us to our senses.

This is the gospel as revealed by Jesus and as conveyed by Paul and all the other Bible writers. Only this takes into account all the relevant facts. Only in this gospel do all the truths revealed about God fit together. The gospel of the cross (of God's righteousness credited to us by Christ our substitute) has within it all that the Bible actually says about love and power.

Love and power are here

It was love that took Jesus to be our substitute on the cross. It was love that called us to repent and warned us of the consequences of refusing. It was love that moved him to commission his disciples to tell the world this message. All this was God's love, vast as the ocean.

It was by God's power that Jesus said: 'No-one takes [my life] from me, but I lay it down of my own accord' (John 10:18). It was by God's power that Jesus could rise from the dead and ascend in triumph to heaven. It was by that power that he is bringing many children to glory (Hebrews 2:10). Indeed, the gospel message itself *is* the power of God to save (Romans 1:16–17). It does not need extra or other dynamic; it does not need to be followed or completed by some show of power; it does not need additional 'ministry' to bring it home. In itself it *is* God's power to save – not just to enlighten or influence, but to save.

All this is relevant to the proper desire to understand all we can of our Christian lives. It is only this gospel that takes into account all the realities of life: the character of God, our state and need, what Jesus did on the cross, what kind of people God is after. As we shall see, other views, though plausible, actually lose touch with, or even deny, some of these realities.

Again and again this amazing gospel brings us back to sanity. This is, incidentally, the fundamental meaning of the term 'evangelical' – holding to and held by the Bible's gospel.

The cross: getting the picture

The Bible has much more to say about the cross of Christ. It brings us other descriptions and illustrations, further images and angles on Christ's once-for-all work. The question is: do they fit together and, if so, how?

Some think them simply so many separate 'models'; we can follow the one that appeals to us and leave the others. Or we can run with the one (say, reconciliation) that seems to resonate most with our broken generation. Is there an overall perspective that we can find?

The Bible shows that all these explanations are vital to give us God's complete picture. They are interlocking truths. They are not like isolated, free-standing articles, but like successive chapters that build into the total story. They have a unity and coherence in presenting what Christ did.

We have seen Christ's death as a 'sacrifice of atonement' (Romans 3:25), the act by which he turned away the wrath of God. This is 'propitiation', meaning that God is now favourable or propitious to us because of the cross. He shows his favour or grace because of Christ taking our place, standing in for us, being our proxy or substitute. 'For Christ died for sins once for all, the righteous for the unrighteous, to bring you to God' (1 Peter 3:18). 'God [sent] his own Son ... to be a sin offering' (Romans 8:3).

Then we have other ways in which Christ's work is described. One is from the law court, with God the Judge and we the guilty. This is *justification*; 'since we have been justified through faith, we have peace with God through our Lord Jesus Christ' (Romans 5:1, see also

3:26). This means that God sets his righteousness to our account and declares us to be acquitted. He says we may walk free out of the condemned cell.

A second description comes from the family. We were once separate from Christ, excluded from God's family (Ephesians 2:12). But 'he predestined us to be *adopted* as his children through Jesus Christ' (Ephesians 1:5). He took us into his family and gave us the Spirit of adoption, so that we can now cry: 'Abba, Father [Daddy]'. Being adopted we become 'heirs of God and co-heirs with Christ' (Romans 8:15–17). 'Justification is the basic blessing, on which adoption is founded; adoption is the crowning blessing, to which justification clears the way,' writes J. I. Packer in *Concise Theology* (IVP, 1993), p. 167.

A third description is from the sphere of relationships. The Bible shows us to be opposed to God and in conflict with him, and so talks of Christ achieving *reconciliation* between God and us. When 'we were God's enemies, we were reconciled to him through the death of his Son' (Romans 5:10). God 'reconciled us to himself through Christ' (2 Corinthians 5:18). The warring parties are brought together.

A fourth is drawn from imprisonment or slavery, maybe with the memory of Israel's bondage in Egypt in mind. We were captured and ensnared by sin, because we had broken God's law. We needed deliverance, someone to set us free. 'Christ *redeemed* us from the curse of the law by becoming a curse for us' (Galatians 3:13). 'We have redemption through his blood, the forgiveness of sins' (Ephesians 1:7). 'Christ has set us free' (Galatians 5:1).

A fifth is taken from the battlefield. We were defeated

by sin, losing the struggle against its pervasiveness, and subject to death. 'Thanks be to God! He gives us the *victory* through our Lord Jesus Christ' (1 Corinthians 15:57). 'Having disarmed the powers and authorities, [Christ] made a public spectacle of them, triumphing over them by the cross' (Colossians 2:15). His resurrection was the ultimate victory.

Some writers have been happy to accept terms like reconciliation or victory, thinking that they do not involve belief in the personal wrath of God. They object to the idea of justification before the Judge and think 'penal substitution' immoral and offensive. They question how one person can justly take another's punishment; they see this view as setting one person of the Trinity against another, as if the Father wants to condemn us and the Son wants to save us and the only solution was for the Father to send the Son to destruction.

Not so at all. As James Denney wrote in *The Death of Christ* (Tyndale Press, 1951): 'In this case the law-giver, the one sinned against, the Judge and the victim are one and the same. If people protest that it is immoral for God to punish our sins as an innocent third party, they have jettisoned the incarnation.' The Father and the Son are absolutely and from eternity at one in plan and purpose in accomplishing our redemption.

So how do the various descriptions of the cross relate? They all rest on and spring from 'Christ in our place'. If Christ had not stood in our shoes, accepted our penalty and acted as our substitute, these other blessings and effects would wither at source. The Bible does give us a 'whole picture' of the cross, as the references below to Isaiah help to show.

- There could be no possibility of our acceptance if the Lord had not 'laid on him the iniquity of us all' (Isaiah 53:6) to secure our justification.
- None of us could ever have been adopted as a child of God, one of his offspring, had the Lord not made his life 'a guilt offering' to bear our iniquities (Isaiah 53:10–11).
- There could be no reconciliation, no relationship with God, if 'the punishment that brought us peace' had not been upon him (Isaiah 53:5).
- There could be no release from the prison of sin, no forgiveness, if Christ had not been 'pierced for our transgressions and crushed for our iniquities' (Isaiah 53:5).
- There could be no victory for us if Christ had not first been stricken 'for the transgression of my people' (Isaiah 53:8), so that 'the will of the LORD will prosper in his hand' (Isaiah 53:10).

All the infinite, irreversible and eternal benefits of Christ's cross rest on that death being for us, in our place. This truth is central and indispensable to everything that Christ did. Take it away and the whole edifice of salvation would fall; Isaiah 53 and many New Testament passages would have to be erased. See it in its fundamental central place, however, and all these blessings become effective to us through the amazing grace of God.

'He poured out his life unto death, and was numbered with the transgressors. For he bore the sin of many, and made intercession for the transgressors' (Isaiah 53:12). That is why Christians who begin to see the significance of the cross live the rest of their lives overwhelmed by grace and overflowing in gratitude.

These truths transform lives, as they did for C. T. Studd, the England cricketer who became a missionary. He had been living a double life, keeping himself back from full commitment to Jesus. But, 'When I came to see that Jesus had died for me, it didn't seem hard to give it all up for him. It just seemed common, ordinary honesty ... if Jesus Christ be God and died for me, then no sacrifice can be too great for me to make for him' (*C. T. Studd and Priscilla* by Eileen Vincent [Kingsway, 1988], pp. 12, 42).

5
Avoiding false starts

The Bible is very clear and precise in the way it presents the gospel to us. Every aspect of that gospel is crucial: its view of God, of us, of the remedy and of the outcome. Underplay or overplay any of those elements and the gospel can be changed subtly. Unfortunately, there is sometimes confusion or vagueness about the gospel even within the church.

Perhaps the most widely accepted variation on the gospel theme is 'the gospel of love': 'We're here to tell others that God loves them'; 'We've come with the message of God's love'; 'Smile, Jesus loves you'; 'The bottom line: God loves you'; 'God has a wonderful plan for your life'; 'God is good and will never stop loving you'; or the church notice-board that carried this assurance: 'Lonely? God's promise: "I will never leave you." '

The main message

No doubt about it, God is love (1 John 4:16). The Bible's evidence of the love of God is pervasive and overwhelming, but what happens when 'God is love' becomes the whole message? Unbelievers hear that the almighty God, maker of the universe, loves them as they are and for ever, with no qualification or call for our response.

One recent advocate of this view expressed it like this: 'Love is the first and the last thing about God.' Not many of us would put it so boldly, to exclude any element of accountability to God. But for many, in practice, the gospel begins with 'the love of God'. That feels like a good message to present; after all, who could take offence at being loved? So 'God is love' becomes the starting-point, as though the Christian message begins with 'The love of God is being revealed from heaven.'

What's the problem? The view of the human condition that follows from this idea of God is not primarily that we have offended God, but that we are strangers to love, needing to be loved, blind to love. We do not first need to repent or change our stance to God, but what we most need is to receive. It is not so much that we are under judgment, though we are foolish and headstrong, like the prodigal son. But like him, we are lonely in the universe, outside the reach and embrace of love. Therefore we feel alone, anxious, unsatisfied, unwanted and fearful.

So, in this view, what's the answer? The remedy is that we need to realize that we are loved, to experience that love and thus find our acceptance. We have to receive his love and release our love to him, to feel his touch and be affirmed.

The outcome of this view is people who feel loved and valued. People who rejoice that 'God loves me', who look to see God's love made evident in their current circumstances. Their focus is that God loves them – in the present – and that he will always go on doing so.

This is an attractive approach. What are its implications?

If God loves us, then fundamentally life is on a good basis. When a child does something stupid or disobedient, words are spoken by a parent, but it normally ends up: 'Daddy/Mummy still loves you and it is all right.' 'God loves you', as the prime element in the gospel, tends to the conclusion that deep down, at the end of the day, all will be fine. Ideas of judgment do not sit easily with this approach, so it is not surprising that some drop them or never mention them. God is good and we will be all right.

The cross, of course, is the great demonstration and proof of his love. 'Greater love has no-one than this, to lay down one's life for one's friends' (John 15:13). He loved us enough to die for us. From this standpoint, however, the cross is not primarily the act of a moral God who finds us guilty, but of a loving God who welcomes us home. This is why, on this view, it is not easy to see the connection between the cross and the love. Why did Jesus need to *die*, after all? He had shown his love all through his life, welcoming tax-collectors and other rejects of society, receiving Samaritans and Romans and women. That was all love; the cross may have shown a greater degree of love, but it was not different in kind. On this view, taken to extremes, the cross could even have been unplanned or a mistake, with human wickedness pushing Christ to death as victim, not victor.

James Denney, in his classic *The Death of Christ*, used the illustration of someone jumping off a pier into the stormy sea 'to show his love for us' … and drowning. His sacrifice was totally unconnected to any need or emergency in our life. It was very loving, but quite pointless. We were still standing safe on the pier. If, however, *we* were in the waves and drowning and he jumped in to rescue us at the cost of his own life, then that *is* love. The act of love made the connection with our situation: he *did* something indispensable; he rescued us.

To change the illustration, if a person's house is catching fire, the first message they need to hear in their danger is: 'Get out – alive.' To talk of love at that point is indisputably well-intended; but if (as the Bible says) they are in eternal danger, that may inadvertently confirm them in the delusion that all is well. Such a message of love, though popular, will prove very unloving if it has the opposite result to the one intended.

This view is loudly silent about judgment; and the Christian message will make little sense if everyone will be OK in the end, whether they repent or not. If evil goes unpunished to the last, we live in a senseless, amoral world under a morally indifferent God. Life will not make much sense if it depends on the love of God giving us 'a good life', since the Bible and history are full of believers who had very tough lives. A friend told me recently that, in the wake of several happy events, he had told another Christian: 'God has been really good to me recently.' The other Christian surprised him by replying: 'That's heresy! Is God good only when things are going well?' If our gospel leads us to believe we will have 'the good life', then we will be hard put to make sense of life when we do not see or feel God's love.

Feeling good

It will also be hard to see sense if we view the gospel as the ultimate 'therapy'. Such a view is not surprising in an age taken over by the many forms of therapy. This *view of God* is that he loves us, wants us to have a wonderful life and to feel good about it. Our *human problem* is that we are blind to him, not realizing all that he wants to give us. The *solution* is to wake up, realize his great love and by faith claim what he offers. Then the *outcome* will be the 'feel good' factor in our lives, as we enjoy all his promises (even to health and wealth) in our experience.

Some forms of church life unknowingly adopt such an approach. The small group is not convened to look seriously at the Bible and apply it, but to help members constantly to feel good – about themselves, about life. The larger meeting is not so much to teach people and prepare them for service as to give them a corporate ecstasy so that they go away at ease in themselves.

Sometimes the focus of conversion or other testimonies is more on 'What God is doing (*i.e.*, what I feel he is doing) in my life' than on what he did once for all on the cross.

Astonishing absence

However, 90% of what 'the gospel of love' affirms is true. Hundreds are strangers to love and God is love. But here, to me at least, is an astonishing statement: the good news, as recorded in the gospels and the Acts, never contains the word 'love'. The term most familiar to us to epitomize the gospel never once appears. (The possible exception is John 3:16, where it is a question of whether the verse was actually spoken to Nicodemus or forms part of John's background commentary.) Jesus speaks much to his disciples of his love for them (*e.g.* John 13 – 17), but not to non-Christians. He looked at the rich young ruler with sadness 'and loved him', but he did not say that to him (Mark 10:21).

This absence of the proclamation of love is stunning. I refused to believe it when someone pointed it out to me, but

I did a check. We all need to do the same. The gospel in the gospels is what Jesus began with: Mark 1:14–15. There is no good news without repentance before the king; no good news without coming to terms with a holy God. 'Repent' is a totally confrontational demand; it is not an invitation to reflect or adjust, but to admit we need a total change, or face the consequences. 'Repent' carries a warning of judgment. There is no suggestion that all is fine. It implies that God has a terrible conclusion for our lives if we do not repent. And chiefly, there is no good news for anyone without believing in Jesus. We need to know all this if we are to appreciate the good news of what Jesus came to bring.

If we say less about the love of God and more about his holiness and hatred of sin, we will say *more* when we do speak of his love.

The 'gospel of love', as it is frequently expressed, does not do justice to the gospel as it comes directly from Jesus. This is also true in the Acts, in the evangelism of the first Christians. This 'love' approach blurs or denies too many truths about God and ourselves to be credible. It skates over such crystal-clear Bible truths as the holiness and wrath of God, the fact that he will bring everyone to account, and the fate of the lost. Love degenerates into affection and sentiment when it is separated from God's justice.

If we start with this approach, our ongoing Christian lives will never add up. At times we will feel guilty, lack assurance and be uncertain of our hope; this teaching will not be able to help us then, since it neglects the basis of our acceptance.

The place of power

Another variant of the Christian message emphasizes

power, as though the gospel begins with the assertion: 'The power of God is being revealed from heaven.' Just as there is no doubt that God is love, so there is no disputing that he is all-powerful. The Bible overflows with evidence of this: it is there from the creation through the cross and resurrection and on to the climax of history. Jesus' life had power all through it.

Every believer knows something of the power of God. We are Christians at all only because of his 'incomparably great power for us who believe. That power ... he exerted in Christ when he raised him from the dead' (Ephesians 1:19–20). It is only because Christ triumphed over the powers by the cross that we are forgiven (Colossians 2:15).

Christians, however, have sometimes misunderstood God's power. Some, for example, have so emphasized God's total control that they have more or less cancelled our responsibility. 'Sit down, young man. When God wants to convert the world, he will do it without your help.' That was the rebuke handed out to the young William Carey when he proposed to discuss world mission at a ministers' meeting in 1792. The older minister rightly believed in God's power, but seriously misapplied it. Thankfully, William Carey ignored his advice and became the first missionary to India.

Many Christians give prominence to power because they passionately want to see God changing people – a high motive, but with a distinctive view of God. Some teach that God and the whole universe must be seen primarily in terms of a power struggle. Unremitting cosmic warfare is going on throughout history in the heavenly places and on earth between God and the devil and all his demons; between good and evil. The devil has his strongholds.

Hierarchies of demons control territories. The powers of evil hold people captive. Against all this God has to bring his power, and to adapt his plans as things go along.

In this view, God does not even know the future – he cannot, for it has not yet happened. He is not the sovereign God in minute control of everything. History looks like the clash of the Titans, the outcome appearing uncertain between God and Satan and depending on how much God's people pray. In some sense his plans are at risk; it is difficult to see how he will win in the end, though we are told that, somehow or other, he will finish on top. Some take this 'power model' as the overarching *view of God*.

That leads to a view of the *human condition*. We are sinful failures, but first and foremost we are weak, prone to wander, lacking the power to resist the forces of evil, pathetic before temptation. We are unable to cope with the devil and his minions, unable to do what we want for God. We are defeated.

We face the personal power of darkness. We need to be able to identify demons, to discover their spheres of operation, to uncover their hierarchies. We need God's power to release ourselves and others. We need to claim the ground and march forward. Because most of us are novices in these matters, we need those who can initiate us into this spiritual warfare.

Deliverance

So, what is the *solution*? We need power and this is what we have in Christ, the victor. He overcame the devil and all his works on the cross and can now, by his Spirit, give us that resurrection power. This means that we can experience God in a supernatural way, as we understand spiritual warfare. We can expect unusual manifestations. God will give works as well as words, experiences as well as expositions. The remedy is to open our heart to the Lord, to pray and to let his power flow. Thus will God deal with defeat and despair. His power encounters will see us through. Essentially we need deliverance.

Then, the *outcome* is life on a new and higher plane, life in the supernatural. We can expect to see everyone healed, any territory freed, providing we have enough faith. The Christian life is lifted above the 'ordinary' into a sphere which the initiated, the spiritual, can enter. Ecstasy and the extraordinary are the order of this new day, as we deal with the realities of the unseen spirit world.

God at risk?

So what does Scripture make of this? Although this approach talks so much of power, strangely it actually tends to cast doubt on God's power. Some writers talk of elements of risk and uncertainty about God's power; he does not have power over every detail. His plans can be thrown, at least temporarily. It is as though we have the power; only if *we* pray will the powers be defeated. God works by response, not by his plan or initiative. He does not so much act as react.

This view comes close to seeing God and the devil as more or less equals, now one having the edge, then the other. The cosmic conflict may turn (as some powerful 'Christian' novels have suggested) not on God's plans and power, but on whether Christians pray enough. If Christians slip, the devil is in and God, for the moment at least, is out.

The Bible knows nothing of such a dualistic universe.

This is God's world. The devil certainly has power, great power, but is always 'on a chain', able to do only what God allows when God allows it. The book of Job is the classic exposition of the power and the limits of the devil in a world that is always God's world (Job 1 – 2).

These views simply do not fit with the Bible's view of God as almighty. He is one from whom and through whom and to whom are all things (Romans 11:36), the one who 'does as he pleases with the powers of heaven and the peoples of the earth' (Daniel 4:35). In the Bible God means God; either he is or he is not.

What is spiritual warfare?

Such a view of God's power also seriously misrepresents the Bible's view of spiritual warfare, as two examples will begin to show. 'Demolishing strongholds' in Paul's mind was demolishing 'arguments and every pretension that sets itself up against the *knowledge* of God'. Paul's weapons were in the realm of 'taking captive every thought ... to Christ'; they were the weapons of truth, of true ideas against false (2 Corinthians 10:4–5). When Paul wrote his classic passage on spiritual warfare, the armour was truth (the belt), righteousness (the breastplate), the gospel of peace (the footwear), faith (the shield), salvation (the helmet) and the Word of God plus prayer. This concluding 'warfare prayer' was not about territories or deliverance or spiritual mapping, but 'that I will fearlessly make known the mystery of the gospel' (Ephesians 6:10–20). Making the gospel known is at the heart of spiritual warfare.

Even more serious, however, is the fact that no amount of power on its own can deal with sin's guilt, penalty and condemnation. Guilt needs atonement, a penalty needs payment, condemnation needs a just acquittal. All those are terms that have to do with a Judge and with justice. God the Judge showed his acceptance of the cross by raising Jesus in power, but the sacrifice of the cross had to come first.

Power can deal with weakness or impotence; only a sacrifice can deal with guilt. God is inexpressibly powerful, but the human dilemma before God could not be resolved by the mere display of power. By his power he spoke a world into being, but he could not simply pronounce a world forgiven. Forgiveness needed a basis before a moral God. Power alone could not be the broker in that situation. As with the 'gospel of love', this approach is simply inadequate to meet the fundamental human need. Moreover, an over-great power emphasis is liable to cross out any theology of suffering (more on this later).

Much of the 'not making sense' feeling in our Christian lives can be traced back to well-meaning but defective views of the gospel. The gospel itself ties together all the realities about God and us, about time and eternity. It shows us that we were guilty before God and totally undeserving of anything but rejection and condemnation. It is a gospel of unmerited favour. This sets the tune for the whole of our subsequent Christian lives: we deserve nothing from God, we have no claim on him in ourselves. If life is tough, we have no ground of complaint. If we receive anything good, it is purely out of his grace. That is the Christian's mindset from the start: no place for self-pity, only for gratitude that Jesus took our place in death.

That is where the Christian life begins. Where does it end?

My Saviour

We have looked at what God has said about the death of his Son. Maybe we could find time to reflect on what Jesus did for us on the cross by reading, unhurriedly and more than once, Luke's account of his death (Luke 22 onwards), then these verses below, as a way of expressing our deep gratitude that even I may 'sing my Saviour's name'.

A purple robe, a crown of thorn,
a reed in his right hand;
before the soldiers' spite and scorn
I see my Saviour stand.

He bears between the Roman guard
the weight of all our woe;
a stumbling figure bowed and scarred
I see my Saviour go.

Fast to the cross's spreading span,
high in the sunlit air,
all the unnumbered sins of man
I see my Saviour bear.

He hangs, by whom the world was made,
beneath the darkened sky;
the everlasting ransom paid,
I see my Saviour die.

He shares on high his Father's throne
who once in mercy came;
for all his love to sinners shown
I sing my Saviour's name.

© 1968 Timothy Dudley-Smith

6
Citizens of heaven

The Christian life presents us with many questions, such as what it means to be human, how to cope in an imperfect world, how to pray, how to relate faith to work, how to promote justice or what church is for. Before we plunge into these here-and-now issues, however, the Bible urges us to look where we are going. We need to look back to the cross and ahead to Christ's coming if we are to get our Christian life in balance from day to day. So we jump ahead to read the last chapter of the story, to look at heaven. We will understand life only if we look to its consummation.

Allan Bloom, in his secular book *The Closing of the American Mind* (Touchstone Books, 1987), said this:

Man has always had to come to terms with God, love and death. Those made it impossible to be perfectly at home on earth. But we are coming to terms with them in new ways. God has been slowly executed; it took 200 years, but theologians tell us he is now dead. His place has been taken by 'the sacred'.

Love was put to death by psychologists. Its place has been taken by sex and meaningful relationships. That has taken only about 75 years.

A new science, thanatology (or death with dignity) is on the way to putting death to death … All one has to do is forget about eternity or blur the distinction between it and temporality: then the most intractable of man's problems will have been resolved. We are learning to 'feel comfortable' with God, love and even death.

A relentless tide

The Bible sees everything about the present in the light of eternity, but a relentless tide of earth-bound ideas has buried the idea of heaven. Evolution saw only this world getting better. To existentialists all that mattered was authenticating ourselves in the present. Secularists and now post-modernists deny humans any ultimate significance beyond this life. To materialists what we have now is all that counts. For pop singers: 'There's no future, just this moment.' Hedonists live for pleasures in the present. To politicians the overriding problem is the current economy and what money can buy. 'The future's not what it used to be', as Woody Allen said.

In the end, many in the church capitulate to this anti-heaven diatribe and limply offer Christianity as a truly human and meaningful life now. Since we are designed to find our ultimate fulfilment in God, it is not surprising that these views do not satisfy. An undefined sense of the spiritual emerges to fill this vacuum, even though that spirituality is as likely to make gods of us, New-Age style, as to think beyond death. If it thinks into the next life, it is likely to be through astrologers, mediums or contact with the dead, or in terms of reincarnation, rather than to have thoughts of judgment or heaven.

No approach could be further from Christianity and yet it eats away at our Christian foundations. This debunking of heaven has a debilitating effect. It pushes us towards this-worldly attitudes. It inclines us towards instant gratification and makes waiting for something seem dated and futile. It turns wishes into longings and longings into needs: 'I need a break', 'I need a new car.' Needs are self-justifying.

A debilitating effect

As we have seen, some current Christianity puts up its own version of what we can claim now. This would attract us much less if we had a true view of heaven. Of course, we still believe in it, but what we are left believing in is very weak and vague. The real world is the one we can see – tangible, material, physical, actual; heaven is spiritual – that is, less real, less solid. If we even half believe that, the devil has scored a major victory. Nothing could be further from the truth. The Bible, particularly the last book, Revelation, teaches many glorious truths about heaven.

1. Heaven is real

It is not imagination or fantasy. It is there. It was from heaven that Jesus came to become flesh (John 1:14; 6:38). It was to heaven he returned, ascending bodily to the right hand of the Father (Acts 1:9). Heaven is where Jesus is, as the Lamb who was slain, still showing in his body the marks of his execution (Revelation 5:6). Heaven is where he is, interceding for us (Romans 8:34). Heaven is as real as he is.

One day, in their resurrected bodies, those whose names are written in the Lamb's book of life will enter it (Revelation 21:27). The real, substantial 'first heaven and first earth' will pass away, to be replaced by a new heaven and a new earth (Revelation 21:1). That realm of existence is the substance; earth, by comparison, is insubstantial, the 'shadow of what is in heaven' (Hebrews 8:5). The present created order will be destroyed, but 'we are looking forward to a new heaven and a new earth, the home of righteousness' (2 Peter 3:10–13).

Heaven has a weight of glory that makes earth and its troubles seem light or weightless (2 Corinthians 4:17). 'The glory of God gives it light' (Revelation 21:23). In heaven God will make everything new (Revelation 21:4–5). Our troubles here are momentary (2 Corinthians 4:17). Our inheritance, which is kept in heaven for us, can never perish, spoil or fade (1 Peter 1:4). Our earthly 'tent' will be destroyed, but we have a 'building from God, an eternal house in heaven, not built by human hands' (2 Corinthians 5:1). That will be real for ever.

On earth we meet from time to time for the Lord's Supper, the 'feast' that celebrates his cross and anticipates his return; heaven will be a rich and lasting banquet (Luke 14:15–24), the 'wedding supper of the Lamb' (Revelation 19:9).

Harry Blamires wrote:

Nothing could be more *concrete* than the picture of heaven in the Book of Revelation. In John's vision of the New Jerusalem, we have a city of walls and gateways and foundations, its measurements defined with the clarity of a mathematical textbook. This is one of the most crucial corrections that need to be hammered into our heads when we think about life in heaven. Our education is such that many people tend to picture the afterlife as something *less* solid, *less* substantial than our earthly life, an existence in some ethereal and virtually disembodied state. In this respect, much current thinking is topsy-turvy.

The one thing we can with certainty say about life in heaven is that it is *more real* than life on earth. We rightly sing hymns in church about the ever-rolling stream of time bearing us all away, about change and decay in everything around us here; we compare the brief life on earth with its cares and sorrows to the tearless life that knows no ending. Such, of course, is the true Christian perspective – to set our eyes on what has *more substance* than earthly life because it is beyond the power of time to wither and destroy.

Christian teaching does not represent the afterlife in terms of what is attenuated and intangible. Christ's imagery of heaven speaks of a place where treasured objects can no longer be consumed by moths and eroded by rust. The *biblical imagery* of harvests and wedding feasts, Abraham's bosom and fiery torment, compels us to grapple with concepts far removed from what is vaporous or nebulous.

Physical religion

Heaven is not a vague spiritual state of being for disembodied spirits; it is the place of those who, through the resurrection of the body, will join him who first rose bodily from the dead and ascended into heaven. Heaven is where the glorified bodies of believers go. Christianity thus is the most physical religion on earth, and in heaven, since it involves bodily resurrection. In the resurrection the body God gave us will be changed (as we shall see next), but it is a body all through, before and after the resurrection. Where else could bodies go than to an equally real place? This is the ultimate point of the Holy Spirit's work of restoring humans to the image of God: that project, begun when Christ formed us, will be consummated in glory.

2. Heaven is heaven, earth is earth

There is the old and passing order and the new and eternal order (Revelation 21:1). They are not to be confused. Heaven is not earth; earth is not heaven. There is continuity, but also contrast and distinction. We need to know this, so that we know what to expect here and there. We may no more expect heaven on earth, in the full sense, than earth in heaven. But always, if mystified on earth at what is going on, we can say: 'But heaven is coming.' That is realism, not escapism. It is no cop-out, but a conviction based on God's covenant. It is the destiny for which God made us and saved us. He means us to know that, while we pursue our pilgrimage on earth, the best is yet to be, the perfect is still to come, the paralysing pain is not permanent, the tears will be wiped away (Revelation 21:4).

Earth experiences all the imperfections of this present order, but heaven will see everything made perfect, even our bodies. Paul underlines the contrast between heaven and earth by explicit reference to what will happen to our bodies (1 Corinthians 15:42–54). They are now perishable, prone to illness and death; they will be raised imperishable in heaven. Here, because of sin, they will die in dishonour; there they will be raised in glory. Here they will fade away in weakness; there they will be raised in power. The mortal bodies we know on earth will then be clothed with immortality. This contrast will give us the right expectations for our earthly life and for our heavenly.

'Our Father refreshes us on the journey with some pleasant inns, but will not encourage us to mistake them for home' (C. S. Lewis, *The Problem of Pain*).

3. Heaven is home

It is home for the redeemed. Earth is a place we pass through on pilgrimage. Heaven will not be a home for the unbelieving (Revelation 21:8) or for 'anyone who does what is shameful or deceitful' (Revelation 21:27). The dwelling of God will be with his believing people; they *will* be his people and God himself will be with them and be their God (Revelation 21:3). They will see his face (Revelation 22:4). It is those who washed their robes and made them white in the blood of the Lamb who will come out of the great tribulation and into their heavenly home. There they will be before his throne, at ease and at home before the throne of the holy God, because the Lamb is their sacrifice and shepherd (Revelation 4:14–17).

Home at last; a permanent city, with temporary tents in the desert a thing of the past (Hebrews 11:9–10). Our citizenship is in heaven (Philippians 3:20). Our home-country passport has been issued from heaven while we still reside here. Heaven is where we belong; we are not ultimately homeless. Peter tells us that we are 'aliens and strangers in the world' (1 Peter 2:11), as were our fellow believers in the Old Testament period. 'They were longing for a better country – a heavenly one' (Hebrews 11:13–16).

Heaven is a permanent reunion or home-coming, with no more parting (1 Corinthians 15:25–26). The American gospel blues singer, Mahalia Jackson, had a great song about heaven called 'Move on up a little higher'. One verse about heaven says, 'It's always "Howdy, howdy" and never "Goodbye".' Yes, precisely!

We shall be active around our home in heaven, for we shall serve him there (Revelation 22:3); but it is also a sphere of rest, not wearisome labour (Hebrews 4:9–10). Heaven will not be home in 'the Englishman's home is his castle' sense; it will not be our private space into which we escape from others. It will be the family home of all God's children, where we are glad for everyone who is there and everyone is thrilled to be with Jesus.

No wonder that the Christian is homesick for heaven ahead of getting there, for 'if our real home is elsewhere, why should we not look forward to our arrival?' (C. S. Lewis, *Letters to an American Lady*).

Scarcity or abundance?

Heaven will be the home where we rejoice with every other member of God's family in common ownership of everything. On earth, what I own takes meaning from the fact that I own a bigger or smaller something than others, or that I have a something that others don't. If I owned a Van Gogh, its value would relate to its *scarcity*; if everyone down my street owned a Van Gogh, it would not be worth nearly so much. An Olympic gold-medallist glories in the fact that there is only one winner; all the rest lose.

Not so in heaven. It is not only the first to break the

tape who will get the crown; the crown of righteousness will be awarded to Paul *and* to all who have longed for Christ's appearance (2 Timothy 4:8). We will all delight in God together in joyful assembly with thousands upon thousands of angels and the whole church of the firstborn (Hebrews 12:22–23). 'In heaven, value resides in *abundance*', as Harry Blamires wrote. The joy of any experience in heaven will be magnified, not diminished, by the fact that everyone else enjoys it too. God's 'award' will be 'not only to me, but also to all who have longed for [Christ's] appearing' (2 Timothy 4:8).

4. Heaven is perfect

Heaven offers all the positives of life here, without the negatives. It completely removes the 'if only' element of human failing and sin. Here, time has the power to wither; it can make flowers and beauty fade, good intentions evaporate and memories die. In heaven it will be different. Nothing will ever perish, spoil or fade (1 Peter 1:4).

There will be no competitiveness, as we have seen, with all its latent acrimony. There will be no puzzlement about what is going on; all will be clear and good. There will be no injustice: we will see that this life was the probationary period, the opportunity, but that all injustice has now been put right.

These are they who have come out of the great tribulation; they have washed their robes and made them white in the blood of the Lamb …

'Never again will they hunger;
never again will they thirst …

For the Lamb ... will lead them to springs of
living water.
And God will wipe away every tear from
their eyes.'

(Revelation 7:14–17)

Not only will there be no tears; there will be no cause for
any tears.

God is greater

Hard though it is to grasp, there will be no sadness in
heaven. We may sometimes think 'I couldn't be truly
happy if so-and-so is not there', maybe a close friend or
relative who never turned to Christ. God is greater than all
our thoughts. Although we can't explain how, the happiness of the redeemed will be complete. They – we – will be
totally content in all that God has done. We will acknowledge his judgment as not only righteous, fair and
deserved, but also good and glorifying to him. We will see
that none can rob God of glory and we will rejoice in that.
God's judgment does not detract from his character, but
rather enhances it. If there were *no* judgment of evil, *that*
would sully his name.

5. Heaven is God and the Lamb

I saw a Lamb, looking as if it had been slain, standing in the centre of the throne, encircled by the four
living creatures and the elders ... In a loud voice they
sang:

'Worthy is the Lamb, who was slain,
to receive power and wealth and

wisdom and strength
and honour and glory and praise!'

Then I heard every creature in heaven and on earth and under the earth and on the sea ... singing:

'To him who sits on the throne and to the Lamb ...'
(Revelation 5:6, 12–13)

'I did not see a temple in the [heavenly] city, because the Lord God Almighty and the Lamb are its temple ... the Lamb is its lamp' (Revelation 21:22–23); 'the river of the water of life ... [flows] from the throne of God and of the Lamb' (Revelation 22:1). Heaven will be the personal presence of the Father and the Son, made real to us by the self-effacing Holy Spirit.

This is the ultimate perspective on the Christian life. Everything begins to make sense in the light of these realities. We need the long view to eternity in order to see the point of our daily steps along the way. When we remember that our expedition is heading for the final summit, we have less trouble keeping going. That helps us when we are wondering why we are struggling across endless moorland or up dangerous rock-faces. Well, if there is no other point to today's journey, at least it brings us a day's march nearer home.

Tough times

Abraham obeyed and went out, 'even though he did not know where he was going'. It is staggering that the great man of faith had no sense of immediate direction in his life from day to day. It must have seemed aimless. Yet he was looking forward to 'the city with foundations, whose architect and builder is God' (Hebrews 11:8–10). He knew the goal; that kept him obeying from day to directionless day.

All the people of faith had tough times; they did *not* receive the things promised, but they saw them ahead and welcomed them from a distance. 'They were longing for a better country – a heavenly one. Therefore God is not ashamed to be called their God, for he has prepared a city for them' (Hebrews 11:16).

The gospel is essentially good news for eternity. The cross is the achievement for eternity. Our fulness in Christ is to prepare us for eternity. The Spirit in us is the foretaste of eternity. Certainly this life, as the T-shirt logo says, is: 'One performance. No rehearsal.' God means us to live for him to the full here and to use all our energy and devotion in the one life on earth we have. But it is the fact of heaven and hell that gives meaning to earth.

It is sobering and motivating to know that God 'will punish those who do not know God and do not obey the gospel of our Lord Jesus ... on the day he comes to be glorified in his holy people' (2 Thessalonians 1:8, 10). If there is an after-life and a judgment; if there is either being saved or being lost; if the world of substance and reality, weight and glory follows, then there is even more reason to live well for God here. By contrast, if we miss the point here, we miss it for eternity.

Hope of glory

The hope of heaven enables us to serve God so much better on earth. We don't have to try to earn our entry by what we do, which means we are delivered from self-regarding motives. Our destiny has been secured by Christ and his death. All the accusations against us have been answered by our substitute. We have for our resources the fulness of Christ and the power of the indwelling Spirit.

Because we know where we are going, we can be content to suffer injustice or hardship, knowing that this is not the life when final justice is done, but that one day all will be put right. We are secure in God's hands, as we treasure the hope of glory. Hope is a central Christian word, fact and gift. It is not wishful thinking but solid, well-grounded certainty. Without hope, we wither inwardly. With Christian hope, we can run and not grow weary. As Jim Packer writes, 'the New Testament nails down this hope by its repeated assurances that the Lord Jesus Christ, our divine sinbearer and present heavenly Friend, is with us by his Spirit to keep us sane and safe until he returns to recreate the cosmos and lead us all into unimaginable endless glory with himself'. Such hope gives us a true sense of significance and destiny. The corrosion of despair is gone, the adrenalin of hope has come.

Throughout this book we will notice time and again the theme of the permanent in contrast to the temporary, heaven against earth, the then against the now. That theme runs through the whole Bible. With that perspective our life here makes more and more sense. We are heading home.

Meanwhile, we have lives to live and work to do for God here. If we are caught up in the slip-stream of those who are already in heaven, we will want to know what God has said about the Christian life. The rest of this book is about that.

The greatest reunion

Recently I came across the newsletter of a group of Christians who graduated together as far back as 1930. The 'Cambridge Missionary Fellowship' still contains many names, but obviously carries several obituaries. A substantial document, it still appears each year and is a remarkable testimony to God's keeping power and to the foundations laid in the Christian Union.

All the contributors know they are nearing heaven. Two typical contributions read:

We are now in 'residential accommodation', supported by a caring church fellowship, many friends and a loyal family, and looking for the day when we shall be landing safe on Canaan's side.

I have appreciated getting these CMF letters over the years. Now it looks as if the greatest CMF reunion of all is yet to come and will be in Heaven – what a chattering, joyful, fulfilled crowd they all will be! Some, a number, have already arrived, lucky beggars! I can see the Lord saying to them all: 'Well done, you lot, thank you for your service to me on earth, now enjoy entering your rest and your company with me.'

That is the Christian hope.

7
Full resources

The gospel is brilliant in its conception and awesome in its execution – literally. Jesus was supernaturally conceived by the Holy Spirit and naturally born of Mary. He was executed by wicked men, while giving his life by God's set purpose, and all so that he might come into the world and be able to bear the sin of guilty people. Where then does the gospel bring us?

The gospel brings us to Jesus and Jesus to us. The Christian life is 'in Christ' (2 Corinthians 5:17) and is therefore 'a new creation'. Something fresh comes into being when people turn to Christ. They are still Chris Black or Jill White, of the same age, family, job and address. They can still use the same passport photographs. They still have the same IQ, the same background, the same essential temperament, the same aptitudes. They are not suddenly someone else, but the same old people who have now become new as well.

Under new management

What's new? The *ownership* is new: they now confess that they belong to God, their new Master. The *identity* is new: they now know that the most important thing about them is being children and heirs of God. The *status* is new: they are now unconditionally accepted into God's family for ever. The *condition* is new: now they have been 'made alive with Christ'. The *company* is new, now that they are in Christ and included in his people. The *power* to go on with God is new, since Christ is now living in them by his Holy Spirit. The whole perspective is new: they now see life from God's angle, so all their values are being renewed. The *prospects* are new: they now have the eternal life that will run on into heaven and glory.

The old has gone. They no longer claim the right to run their own lives. They know that the old pursuit of 'image' was pathetic. They are no longer under God's wrath, no longer 'dead in transgressions and sins'. No longer out on their own before God, depending on their own hopeless moral energy. The old prospect of hell has been removed.

Where does this leave them and us? We are not what we were, since so much is new; but we are not yet what we will be when we reach heaven. In fact, we are a very long way from perfection. Our frequent failures every day give us sad reminders of that. Only when we see him will we be like him (1 John 3:2).

We are in an in-between position, where we need help – help which comes from and in Christ.

Naïve and gullible

Paul wrote his letter to the Christians at Colosse when they were being enticed to look elsewhere for help. They were a bit naïve when they heard people go 'into great detail about what [they have] seen' in visions (Colossians 2:18). That all sounded very spiritual and they wanted in on it. Some were drawn to human rules and regulations, as though such Do's and Don'ts could help them forward as Christians (Colossians 2:16, 20–23). Paul's concern was to draw his hearers away from all such side-tracks and back to Christ. His letter is brim-full of who Christ is and what he has done, so that he can affirm to them: 'You have been given fulness in Christ' (Colossians 2:10). Christ did not merely give them a start; by the Holy Spirit he gave them fulness.

Who he is

Paul gives us a summary of who Jesus is (Colossians 1:15–20; 2:3, 9). He is the visible likeness of the invisible God, in authority over all creation. Everything was created by him and for him. He existed before everything and holds everything together (if he did not constantly do so, everything would collapse into chaos). All the treasures of God's wisdom and knowledge are hidden in him and God's fulness lives in him in bodily form. What a person!

The point is: we are in that person and he in us. Why do we ever look elsewhere for help? He is and has it all.

What he has done

This is underscored when we read Paul on what Jesus Christ has done (Colossians 1:12–14, 21–22; 2:10–3:3). God has qualified us to share in his saints' inheritance in the realm of light. He rescued us from the power of darkness and installed us under his Son's kingship. In Christ we have redemption, deliverance, reconciliation – the foundational and incomparable favour of the forgiveness of our sins. We can now stand before him, whom to see unforgiven is to die, without blemish and free from accusation. God has cancelled all that stood against us, nailing it to the cross as finished and paid. By the cross he has disarmed Satan and his legions of all their power and authority.

This Christ is in us, the hope of glory. We are complete in him (I repeat, *complete*). We have been raised with Christ to newness of life. Our life is hidden with Christ in God, beyond the reach of harm.

The point again is: we are in Christ, the one with all grace and power and victory. If we have come to him, we have come to fulness. In Christ are all the resources we need.

Fulness and failure?

The problem is, however, that it rarely looks or feels like that. It is very understandable if some come back with a genuine question: 'If you have come to fulness in Christ, why is your life still such a failure? I don't see fulness in your life. You need something more to make you complete.' We have all felt the force of their argument. The Colossian teachers were already using such an argument, proposing various forms of 'something more' to their hearers.

Wanting more

'Lord, there's got to be *more*. This can't be what Jesus died for. Lord, give me more.' All of us find echoes of that in our hearts, a divine discontent at our own weakness and poverty. It is at such moments that we are often urged to 'be open to God; be open to whatever he has for you'. That resonates with our desires for God. We would not want to be closed to God; we hate to be shutting him out of any area of our lives. We want all that he is and offers.

When we reach that depth and cry out for more, we come to possibly the greatest opportunity in the whole of our Christian lives – and, at the same time, to an immense danger. It all depends where we look when we seek more. If we look to Christ, he will surely answer our cry and come to us. If we look for some other experience, we will be ensnaring ourselves and going astray.

Many Christians who start out by genuinely seeking 'more' end up disillusioned and despairing, because they were led to seek more in some unbiblical experience or formula. Maybe they were pressed to look for one overwhelming experience that would lift their life to a wholly new plane. They never found it, because no such single experience exists.

We need to think twice about 'being open' to God. That phrase obviously can have a good intention. I want to be open to whether God wants me to serve in Aberdeen or Afghanistan. I want to be open to my church asking me to help in some new venture. I want to be open to God to use my money, time, energies as he wants. But sometimes 'being open' can mean something different and can even leave us open to what is not from God.

The New Testament does not call us to be 'open' to undefined ideas or experiences. It calls us above all to fix our eyes on Jesus and consider (that is, to think hard about) him and what he endured (Hebrews 12:2–3). It gives us many examples of what to seek from God, not only in its direct teaching about the Christian life, but also and particularly in the prayers it sets before us. Rather than 'being open' to the latest experience (which is often what the phrase means in practice), we do much better to take a New Testament prayer and make it our own. One such is in Colossians 1:9–14: 'asking God to fill you with the knowledge of his will through all spiritual wisdom and understanding ... [to] live a life worthy of the Lord ... bearing fruit ... being strengthened ... so that you may have great endurance and patience, and joyfully [give] thanks ...'

'Being open' often suggests shutting our minds off and letting it happen, whatever 'it' turns out to be. That is never God's way. A prayer like Paul's combines mind (knowledge, understanding), heart (joy, thanks), will, experience, obedience and practical outworking, and brings us back to 'the Son he loves, in whom we have redemption, the forgiveness of sins'.

We need to look for more in the right place and in the right way.

Paul's cautions

This is why Paul gave specific warnings to the Colossians. Some warnings were against being too spiritual. Don't let anyone take you captive through plausible ideas that sound spiritual but are merely human. Don't be impressed by those who boast of visions. Don't let the super-spiritual make you feel second-class.

Other warnings were against becoming legalistic. Don't let anyone set rules for you where Scripture does not (in their case, on what to eat, when or where to meet, and so on). Don't be under anyone's judgment where God has set you free. (See Colossians 2:8, 16, 18, 20.)

The pressures that came to the Colossians still come to us. We can be tempted in the same two directions: to be over-spiritual or to be legalistic (or both at once). In the first direction we may be tempted to flaunt our freedom, to claim special experiences, to seek a hot-line to God. In the other direction we may be drawn to conform to the unwritten rules of our church or group about dress, language, Bible versions or behaviour. The super-spiritual route and the legalistic one both end up by bringing people into bondage. 'Experiences' may seem to offer freedom and 'rules and regulations' to offer security, but they both enslave their adherents.

Not two stages

We can resist these temptations if we see what happens when someone becomes a Christian. Whether a conversion is abrupt or gradual, what happens is a coming out of death into life, out of darkness into light. The person is no longer condemned, but accepted; no longer on his or her own, but with the Holy Spirit within as his or her permanent houseguest. A line has been crossed; *the* line that settles our eternity. That experience ushers us *into* God's family; all subsequent experiences are *within* that family. Through one action of God we become God's children and heirs of heaven; all later experiences are to do with how we grow as God's children.

Having crossed the line, there will be many stages in our Christian development, but there is no one single experience that we have to seek. It is not that first comes a 'Jesus experience', to be followed by a 'Holy Spirit experience'. 'The Spirit of him who raised Jesus' – and us – 'from the dead *is* living in you', Paul told the Roman Christians; 'you received the Spirit of adoption … The Spirit himself testifies with our spirit that we are God's children' (Romans 8:11, 15–16).

If we have come to Christ, even if we have come to

Christ only today, we have fulness in him; that is the description of the basic believer (Colossians 2:10). God may, indeed will, give us many experiences: a second, a third, a fourth, a one hundred and fourth; that is in his gift. This may be so with particular force if we have lapsed in our walk with God or drifted into ungodly ways. We may then find the experience of God restoring us to forgiveness and the joy of our salvation almost like another conversion. If so, praise God for restoration. But ultimately praise him that we are in the family in the first place.

Play up, play down

If we find an emphasis on one second experience as a must for becoming filled, we need to beware lest we find ourselves thinking of our initial experience: 'It was "just conversion", just the start. I didn't really know much then. I was still a failure. Now I've come to a deep experience of God for the first time.'

It may well be that some of us were converted very quietly and gradually (I was), so that we scarcely noticed a cross-over day; or that, when we were converted, the message we heard was very thin and gave us a weak start. In either case we need to learn more of the gospel. But the start of the Christian life is in itself cataclysmic – a transfer from condemnation to acceptance, from Satan to God, from hell to heaven. Nothing must down-play its significance. It is the change which settles eternity. It is better to spend time unpacking that change than seeking some other experience.

In any case, no single experience, however deep, will see us through life. No second experience, whatever its attendant gifts, will lift us above weakness and temptation for the rest of our lives. The higher the claims for such an experience, the more the let-down days or months later. No such 'get me there' experience is promised. What is offered is all the fulness of Christ, to be sought, appropriated and enjoyed each day in whatever opportunities or trials may come. Forget the quick fix. Go for the fully resourced, long-haul expedition with Christ. In a lifelong pilgrimage what will help us most is not some amazing encounter in year two, but a deepening relationship to the one who is in us and will go with us in his fulness through twenty, thirty, fifty or more years.

We have a long way to go, just as the Colossians did. They were just starting on a lifelong pilgrimage, but they had fulness in Christ. They had the one who had everything. All they could possibly ever need was in Christ. They had no need to go anywhere else for help. What they had to do was stick with Christ, turn to Christ and seek his resources. They had initially and decisively turned to him at the start; now they had deliberately to turn to him continually, every day, in every situation.

What it feels like

The trouble is that 'having fulness' is not what our lives feel like. We feel more empty than full, more failure than success. The great thing is that Paul knew all this when he wrote to the Colossians. He was fully aware of their daily realities. In his mind he was not on cloud 9, but at 9 Market Street, Colosse. He made clear that having fulness in Christ did not mean they were perfect: 'just as you received Christ Jesus as Lord, continue to live in him, rooted and built up in him, strengthened in the faith as you were taught ...' (Colossians 2:6–7). They needed to go on, to work out Christ's Lordship in every area of life: work, ownership, friends, family, society, and so on. They needed to put down roots and build themselves up, to go on gaining strength from true teaching. They had not arrived. They had to go on putting to death (murdering) whatever belonged to their earthly nature, which was obviously still with them (Colossians 3:5). They had deliberately to put on compassion and other virtues, which were not theirs naturally (Colossians 3:12).

Working at it

In other words, it was all in Christ, but they had to work at it. Christian slaves still had problems at work with the temptation to obey only when they were being watched or in order to win favours. Christian masters still had to wrestle with the temptation to exploit their workers. Christian husbands could sometimes be harsh, Christian fathers could lose their cool (Colossians 3:18–4:1). That was the real world; those were the actual Christians. Yet they all had come to fulness in Christ.

Fulness can coexist with the need constantly to be filled – that is, with the fact that we are 'leaky vessels' always tending to run on empty. George Verwer of Operation Mobilisation puts it neatly: 'I know where the free refills are.' Having fulness does not mean that we have arrived, just that in Christ we have everything we need. It is rather like saying: 'The money's in the bank. Draw on it. Don't live in debt. If you don't use it, you won't benefit.'

Fulness can coexist with struggle, as Paul's experience showed. His aim was to 'present everyone perfect in Christ. To this end', he wrote, 'I labour, struggling with all his energy ... I want you to know how much I am struggling for you' (Colossians 1:28–2:1).

We will have times when we look back on some struggles and think: 'Wow! I never thought I'd get through that. I never thought I was strong enough to resist the pressure. I never imagined I could find the words. I never dreamt I could point someone to Christ.' There are times when we know it must have been Christ's fulness, his resources, his strength in our weakness. At such times we can say to God: 'Thank you *so* much for showing me that it is spiritual to struggle.'

Relating to Christ

This truth about our fulness is a great encouragement to relate to Christ: to talk to him, study his life, absorb his teaching, follow his commands, love what he loves, hate what he hates. Fulness is not some mystical experience; not a feeling of hot surges running down our back. It is a life of going on with the Master. That fulness is drawn on as we use (in the classic phrase) the means of grace. Christ has given us the means to know and grow in his fulness and means are vital, as spiritual growth does not happen automatically or on its own. We need to be serious and diligent in using these means. We need to meet with other Christians, to hear God's Word opened and applied, to be regularly at the Lord's Supper, to be getting to know the Bible, to be spending time in conversation with God, to be avoiding needless exposure to temptation, to be confessing and turning from sin.

God will surprise us

So Paul's thrust is this: keep drawing on your resources in Christ. Don't waste time looking for some alternative way.

God will give us intimate experiences of his presence at many points in life, particularly in times of suffering; he will give them in his own time and often they will surprise us, just as a good human father will plan good surprises for his children. We cannot command them or find a formula for them.

Our responsibility is to receive what God has said about our fulness in Christ and then to relate to Christ and go on using his resources. This is why God sent the Holy Spirit.

The Holy Spirit led the writers of the New Testament into all his truth (John 14:17) and now works to open our eyes to what is in Christ for us (John 14:26). He affirms to us our adoption, that God is actually our Father and we his children and heirs (Romans 8:15–17). He gives us the inner power and resolve to live with and for Christ – and, through it all, pours out his love into our hearts (Romans 5:5). The more the Spirit works, the more he is self-effacing, the more he puts Christ in the centre. He does not want attention for himself; he wants that to focus on Jesus (John 15:26; 16:12–15).

Hungry, but satisfied

If we genuinely know Jesus Christ, if we have grasped the salvation that he achieved for us, we will be content. We will feel our own weaknesses, but know we lack nothing. We will be hungry for more of God, wanting to know him better, but not itching for some extra experience or some higher light. We will know that we are on a long pilgrimage, but will be trusting the resources of Jesus Christ and taking each day in his company as it comes.

A severe case of SBD

The date was 56 AD. A group of young Christians in a town called Colossae (in modern-day Turkey) had a real problem. It was the problem of SBD – and it threatened to affect the church in a, well, colossal way. Its members were new-ish Christians wanting to please God and know him more and more. Then SBD struck. And these Christians got confused and worried.

SBD became so serious that the apostle Paul, who was in prison, thought he'd better write to warn them about SBD and to encourage them to get going again.

SBD stands for Subtle but Dangerous. What it amounted to for the Colossians was a case of 'Jesus Plus'. A bit like this:

'There's got to be more to this Christianity lark than just forgiveness, living God's way and heaven!'

'I used to be a run of the mill Christian, but then I went to a meeting, got zapped and now everything is really cool.'

'Just follow these simple rules and your Christian life will be transformed.'

'What we need is a Christianity that focuses more upon what we can experience through meditation.'

Heard stuff like this before? This counts as SBD. All of these options are held by people today and sound attractive. They were to the Colossians, too. They were being told that it was OK to believe in Jesus, but to know God deeply and to please him fully they needed something else. 'I don't think so', said Paul. So he wrote a letter.

Before the arrival of SBD, things were fine. The church had been started by a bloke called Epaphras (anagram: 'Sharp Ape'), who became a Christian when he heard Paul preach in Ephesus and returned to Colossae to tell others about Jesus. They became Christians and the church began.

By looking at Paul's letter, we'll learn not only how to recognize and deal with false teaching, but also what it really means to be a Christian, both in terms of privileges and responsibilities.

You'll find the letter helpful if you're a younger Christian, as the Colossians were. Or if you've been a Christian a bit longer, you'll find the letter a brilliant refresher course and incentive to go on with Jesus, as he wants us to.

The above is taken, by permission, from *The Ichthus File: The Bible Fair and Square*. The File describes itself as 'a whole new approach to unlocking the greatest book of all time – the Bible. It is fast-moving and faith-building. And we think it might even be a little bit funky. Except that we're not quite sure what that means ...'

The 'IF' gives daily but undated readings with accompanying notes/questions. It is published by St Matthias Press and Radstock Ministries. For a free sample copy, send to PO Box 665, London SW20 8RL, phone 0181 947 5686, fax 0181 994 7091 or Email Mattmedia@hotmail.com.

8
Humans being restored

We have looked at fulness in Christ, but what *is* life for the Christian? Masses of questions spring to mind at this point. How exactly does God intend to work on us and in us? How should our life shape up? Has God given us an overall picture, so that we can know what we are aiming for? Or do we just try to do all the bits and pieces (praying, reading the Bible, giving, meetings, witnessing, and so on) and hope it all works out?

We need to find answers to such questions if we are to make sense of our lives along the way. In broad terms, as we have seen, we are likely to meet contrasting pictures of the Christian life.

'Rules and regs'

The first picture is 'rules and regulations' Christianity. This has a long and inglorious history. It is like some weeds; you think you've pulled out the whole root, but always enough remains deep down for the weed to grow again. Legalism keeps coming to the surface. We think that we have to do certain things and not do other things; if we succeed, we are good, spiritual Christians. Such spirituality is not a matter of the heart or of loving God, but of observing the externals. Paul warned the Colossians against 'submitting to rules' such as 'Do not handle! Do not taste! Do not touch!' These, he wrote, are 'human commands and teachings ... [which] have an appearance of wisdom ... but they lack any value in restraining sensual indulgence' (Colossians 2:20–23).

Paul warned Timothy against people who impose 'rules and regs', forbidding marriage or certain foods (1 Timothy 4:3). He warned the Galatians against those who would rob them of their freedom in Christ by burdening them again with a yoke of slavery (Galatians 5:1) and trying to impose a ritual on Christians (Galatians 6:12).

Strong appeal

Legalism has two appealing features. (As Walter Lippmann, the American columnist, said: 'People welcome manacles to prevent their hands from shaking.') One is that legalistic Christians genuinely want their faith to have an impact in every area of their lives. They see that there are many things that God commands us to do. We are to give, to meet together, to pray and read the Bible. We are to pay our taxes, to avoid any appearance of evil, to care for the needy. We could construct a long list of God's commands for Christians. Legalism brings these to our attention; we need to hear them and know that they are God's will.

The other appeal of 'rules and regs' is that we can all keep them. We can all conform, especially when that confers acceptance in our chosen circle. We can all do the outward thing. We can talk, dress, behave, pray in the laid-down way – and we're there. But where?

Fearful bondage

'Rules and regs' are a fearful bondage. They breed pride (if we keep them) or false guilt (if we don't). They make us look over our shoulder at others rather than up to God. They rob us of true joy and peace. They cut us out of Christian freedom. They deprive us of knowing that 'everything God created is good, and nothing is to be rejected if it is received with thanksgiving, because it is consecrated by the word of God and prayer' (1 Timothy 4:4–5). Worst of all, perhaps, legalism makes us essentially self-centred: Am I all right? Have I conformed? Am I accepted? The Pharisees were not noted for thinking of others.

Legalism is no respecter of churches or theologies; it can and does appear anywhere and everywhere. The strictest and the freest of churches, the oldest and the newest are all alike and equally prone to this. (It takes only three weeks for a new fellowship to develop its own incipient rules and regulations.) Weeds grow even faster in better soil.

The spiritual route

The second picture of the Christian life is the exact opposite. It stresses the 'spiritual' rather than the legal, the inward rather than the outward, deliverance rather than mere duty. Spiritual Christians are those who have freedom from Do's and Don'ts and evangelical taboos. They are not fettered by having to conform and do not live life by the book or the letter. They live by the Spirit, moving in a realm of experience above the average. They can, apparently, hear from God, receive visions or words and have insight into what God is doing.

Legalistic Christians seek to do, to perform. The super-spiritual seek to experience, to feel and to flow. Undoubtedly, such spirituality has a strong attraction. It appeals directly to those who 'want more'. It rightly points out that the Christian life is a *life*, not a dreary round of duty. It talks of relationship and intimacy and freedom. It seems to exist on an altogether higher level. The 'spiritual' Christians also want their faith to affect every part of life.

Super-spirituality, in the event, is not all it seems. Not too many make it to those heights, which, it seems, are for the initiated, the leaders, those really in touch with God. A kind of priesthood develops in those who can lift others to the heights of experience. A dependency can creep in; dependency on people rather than on God. An 'inner knowledge' arises, independent of the Bible, which has to be received. Heavy leadership tends to mark such spirituality, together with a tendency always to be seeking the latest great experience.

Back into bondage

In the end, it is as much a bondage as legalism – a bondage to 'freedom'. It shares many of the failings of legalism, becoming very self-regarding. Have I arrived? Have I had the experience? Am I there yet? I, me. The Colossians were simultaneously tempted to super-spirituality and to legalism. No matter that 'people go into great detail' about visions, 'they have lost connection with the Head, from whom the whole body … grows as God causes it to grow' (Colossians 2:18–19).

Legalism 'lacks any value'; super-spirituality stunts growth.

With a human face

The third picture of the Christian life is 'humanity being restored'. 'You have been raised with Christ ... and have put on the new self, which is being renewed in knowledge in the image of its Creator' (Colossians 3:1, 10). Being renewed in the image of God is one of God's basic pictures of our Christian life. On that basis alone does life make sense.

God did not make us robots, which could be programmed to perform certain functions. This reminds us that Jesus did not call us servants – merely to get certain things done – but friends (John 15:15). God did not make us angels, to float through life untouched by the pressures of the earth and the body. He has not forgotten that he made us in his image as human beings. He meant the world to be peopled by human beings; creatures with bodies and minds, memories and emotions, wills and consciences, relationships and abilities.

No Plan B

Then, tragically, sin intervened and fouled up God's creatures and his creation. That, however, did not cancel God's purposes for people. He did not then say: 'Right, we will now forget working with humans (Plan A) and adopt some Plan B.' Rather, as he had long planned, he set about restoring the situation. He sent the man Christ Jesus, 'the image of the invisible God', the one in whose image humans had been made (Colossians 1:15). There, before the world, was what a human was meant to be. As Jesus lived a fully human life, he showed what human nature could and should be. He thought, reasoned, understood. He had experiences, felt emotions. He knew joy and sorrow, compassion and anger.

He walked and climbed (and must have been fit). He became hungry and tired. He had times of rest. He had friendships (and enemies). He remembered, he took decisions. He appreciated beauty, observed creation, gave and received hospitality. He knew and walked with God.

God's purpose now is for us to be 'conformed to the likeness of his Son', Jesus the man (Romans 8:29). That does not mean seeking some mystical state of otherness. It means our humanity being restored towards one day being like his. It means that, as we go on with Christ, we will become more and more truly human. As the Spirit who indwells us works in our lives, his aim is to restore the original, the human.

Not an escape

It is tragic that so often the spiritual life, the life that pleases God, is pictured as an escape from the human, as though human means sinful and spiritual must mean something contra-human. Not so. 'Let us make human beings in our image …'; 'Christ … is the image of God'; we are 'being renewed … in the image of [our] Creator' (Genesis 1:26; 2 Corinthians 4:4; Colossians 3:10). That is the sequence and pattern.

Humanity affirmed

This has revolutionary consequences for us and makes brilliant sense of our lives. It means that God affirms our humanity – not our sin, but our humanity. He is not trying to replace our humanity with 'something higher', but seeking to infuse our humanity with his knowledge, love and power. He wants us to be more human than we were, not less.

He honours our bodies with the promise and hope of bodily resurrection; his ultimate intent is not to have heaven full of disembodied spirits. He honours our minds with the capacity for thought, abstract and concrete, and with the whole revelation of himself in the Bible. (What the Bible has done throughout history to open, stretch and stir the human mind is incalculable.) We are not to be like 'the horse or the mule, which have no understanding' (Psalm 32:9). He honours our wills by showing us the choices that make for his glory and our good. He does not want us to give blind obedience or to be undiscerning slaves. He honours our emotions by showing us the emotions of Jesus, and of the psalm writers and many others.

In other words, our first concern in following God should not be 'How can I become spiritual?' but 'How can I use for God all the human powers and faculties God gave me?' How can we use our mind, memory, will, emotions, body, creativity, ability to relate and so on for him? He does not call us to deny those and set them aside, but to put them into action for him. This is the thrust of Romans 12:1–2. We are not to deny our bodies, but make them over to God (*living* sacrifices) every day. We are not to turn off our minds, but to have them renewed and active.

Crucial issue

This is a crunch issue for us as Christians. All false teaching on the Christian life ends up by dehumanizing us, whether it comes from the legalistic or the 'spiritual' end. This is most obvious in the sects, with members who have handed over their minds and been pressed into a mould. It can happen in churches, too. We have all come across groups where everyone seems the same – where dress and catch-phrases and behaviours and mannerisms conform. It can happen in the best circles, but when it does we can be fairly sure that the teaching is askew. By contrast, all true teaching dignifies the humanity God gave us. God made us humans; he is now restoring us from being fallen humans towards the great day when our humanity will be perfected and we will be like him (1 John 3:2).

How does 'humanity being restored' work out in practice now? Here are some examples:

First, it means that when we want to know God himself, we go to the Bible, use our minds, read seriously and think about it. This is what Paul told young Timothy: 'Reflect on what I am saying, for the Lord will give you insight' (2 Timothy 2:7).

Second, it means that when we want to grow as Christians, we apply our wills, as we make every effort to add to our faith goodness, knowledge, self-control, perseverance, godliness, mutual affection and love (see 2 Peter 1:5–8).

Third, it means that if we want guidance, we should both ask God for wisdom (James 1:5) and also be willing to make up our minds and take decisions on the basis that the mature are '[those] who by constant use have trained themselves to distinguish good from evil' (Hebrews 5:14).

Fourth, it means that, if we find our emotions rising, we will seek to ensure that they spring from understanding and not emotionalism. Anger and compassion, those contrasting emotions, both need to be based on truth, as they were in Jesus. Jesus' anger was aroused because in his mind he perceived stubborn hearts; his compassion was stirred because he understood that the crowds were harassed and helpless (Mark 3:5; Matthew 9:36).

No spiritual drip-feed

God may or may not give specific 'words' or insights or

experiences. He may or may not give a sense of peace that 'this is his will' over a house purchase. Many have felt that he has told them whom to marry. But he has not promised such things and such words do not cut out the need for a surveyor's report or for checking out the other person's character. God can give instant guidance – praise him! Essentially, however, he has given us his Word as sufficient to shape us in our character and outlook. He is not intending to put us on a spiritual drip-feed or to give us continual fixes about his will. He is working to remake us in the true humanity that is his image. His basic pattern is to go on with his restoration work in our humanity. We are to co-operate with him in that, as he works in us, so that we come to choose and to behave according to his good purpose (Philippians 2:13).

Taking steps

This is the only way in which we will grow as Christians. A child learns to walk by taking a step and falling over, not by waiting for the gift of walking. Watch a child who can now walk trying to speak. You can see that some idea is inside and wants to get out, but it is quite a struggle. We learn to think only by thinking, to do by doing. We never develop by doing nothing. Some attitudes to guidance are immaturity dressed up as spirituality. God honours us by not giving us everything 'on a plate'.

Even Jesus the man 'learned obedience from what he suffered' (Hebrews 5:8). The perfect human being could and did learn. He had never before approached death and that experience was new for him. Moreover, he could 'become perfect'; we read that, 'once made perfect, he became the source of eternal salvation' (Hebrews 5:9). He was always the perfect Son of God, but was prepared for his saving role by what he suffered. If the perfect Jesus could learn, how much more can we, the imperfect? If he could be made perfect by what he suffered, how much more does that apply to us in whatever we suffer?

God is busy 'restructuring humanity' and this brings countless benefits. We mention just two of them.

Variety affirmed

God's restructuring endorses variety. In his image God made everyone different. Imagine the wonder it would be if car manufacturers made every car different! In restoring the image, God keeps and enhances the distinctiveness of each one. Other spiritualities tend to press their adherents into a mould – keep the same 'rules and regs' or seek this one common experience. Biblical spirituality encourages as much variety and colour as there are different individuals created by God. No sausage factory this. God wants us, while being restored, to be ourselves. There is no superficial conformism here, but room for all shapes and sizes. That is part of the Christian freedom that is given to those who are being renewed. So let us take care not to judge one another for being different.

Power in weakness

Another benefit of God restoring our humanity is that we experience the power of God. In some circles that power is there only if it zaps people and things are visibly happening. But countless believers can testify that God's power is made perfect in their weakness (2 Corinthians 12:9), in the vulnerability of their human experiences.

When the power of God entered the world in the incarnation, it took the form of a weak and helpless, totally dependent baby. When Jesus walked this earth, he was always vulnerable to plots, denials and betrayal. God's power was shown in Jesus being forsaken on the cross. His power was invested in a bunch of weak, argumentative, unimpressive men. Jesus works through weakness, for his weakness is stronger than human strength. And that strength is given to the believing human beings he is restoring into his image. It is not flamboyant or ostentatious, but works unseen in the mind and heart. The results of that working, of course, can be seen in character and conduct.

That is the picture of the Christian life God wants us to follow, to make sense of all the realities.

What we have been looking at in this chapter is the nature of the spirituality that is taught in the Bible. 'Spirituality' is not necessarily the most helpful term, but is certainly in vogue in secular and religious circles as well as Christian.

Many contrasting spiritualities are followed in an age that has moved beyond cold materialistic logic: eastern, orthodox, catholic, mystical, New Age, contemplative, Celtic, post-evangelical and many more. They all say something about humans having a spiritual aspect or dimension, but some are fundamentally astray. Others may have insights or elements of truth, but each comes from a particular angle, leaving them unbalanced or partial.

Biblical spirituality, the Bible's approach to the Christian life, is radically different. It may not often be very well lived out, but that is our failure, not the Bible's. In itself it covers all the angles of human personality and life. It satisfies the intellect, the will and the emotions. It involves both body and soul. It relates to the past, the present and the future. It covers rest and work, thought and activity. It suits all temperaments. It equally fits men and women, young and old, east and west, educated and uneducated, individuals and communities, rich and poor. It brings us all the things that are truly good that people hope to find in other spiritualities.

Once we can see what God is doing in giving us fulness in Christ and restoring our humanity, we will not need to look for any other spirituality.

Emotions

Did Jesus experience human emotions? It is a crucial question, with huge practical implications.

People have pulled in opposite directions on this issue. Some have so stressed his deity as to make him seem cold, remote and unfeeling. Others have so stressed his humanity as to obscure his dignity as the Son of God.

The gospels show that he had human feelings. For example, he felt hungry and tired. Sometimes he felt like withdrawing to be alone. Beyond such references, four major human emotions shine out in his life.

Compassion is the most frequently mentioned. This was stirred by the need or distress of individuals (two blind men, a leper, and so on) or crowds (the multitude, as sheep with no shepherd). When he felt pity, he acted; he gave help 'with an amount of sympathy that doubled its value'. With the bereaved widow, his 'heart went out to her and he touched the coffin ... the dead man sat up ... Jesus gave him back to his mother'.

Indignation was also part of his emotional life. When the Jews opposed the healing on the Sabbath of the man with the withered hand, Jesus looked round on them in anger and deep distress at their stubborn, insensitive hearts. He was irritated, annoyed or vexed when his disciples rebuked those who were bringing children to him.

The death of Lazarus left him 'deeply moved in spirit and troubled', the words suggesting irrepressible anger, even rage, at death's intrusion. Then there was his incandescent zeal over the commercialization of the temple and the posturing of the Pharisees.

Of course, he was also a man of sorrows and familiar with grief. He knew what it was for tears to flow. He sighed from the bottom of his heart over human wilfulness and obstinacy. He was distressed at the prospect and experience of the cross.

He also experienced joy. He endured the cross because of the joy set before him. He was 'full of joy through the Holy Spirit'. He cannot have proclaimed news of great joy with a long face.

These human emotions were all in the life and experience of Jesus. He is therefore a great comfort to us, as he is able to sympathize with our weaknesses. He is also a great challenge as he shows us what stirred his emotions – not whim or sentiment, but understanding.

He felt compassion because he *understood* the plight of people (lost, in darkness). He became angry because he *saw* the error of the Pharisees and the evil of death. He was moved to joy because he *grasped* what lay beyond the cross. He felt sorrow because he *perceived* what the cross would involve, or what would be the fate of those who rejected him.

Truth prompted and shaped his emotions. It should be the same for us.

The emotions of Jesus are worth further study. The following Bible references may be a starting guide.

Compassion	Matthew 9:36; 14:14; 20:34; Mark 1:41; 8:2; Luke 7:13; 19:41.
Anger	Matthew 15:7; 23; Mark 3:5; 10:14; Luke 13:15; John 2:15–17; 11:33.
Sorrow	Matthew 26:37; Mark 8:12; John 11:35.
Joy	Luke 10:21; Hebrews 12:2.

9
In a broken world

It is just as well that we have such infinite resources in Christ, for we are not only still frail and prone to wander, but we are also still on earth. Though that is stating the obvious, it is often forgotten.

We are not yet in heaven. Heaven, however, does exist and earth stands in contrast to it. Heaven is the realm of perfect well-being, true prosperity and no tears, but we are not there yet. We are still subject to all the ills that flesh is heir to. Earth is the sphere of 'our present sufferings'. The creation is not yet fulfilled, but is waiting eagerly for God's conclusion. That will come when the children of God will be revealed to the watching world and the unseen powers as proof of his grace and power. Meanwhile, the created order, of which we are inextricably part, is in bondage to decay, subject to frustration and groaning as in the pains of childbirth (Romans 8:18–25 sets all this out clearly).

No surprise

All this is a consequence of sin entering the world. It should be no surprise that this is a world of trouble; our newspapers and TV screens report this to us every day.

One question this poses is whether Christians are to expect the same lot in life as unbelievers? Or does God give us a better deal? Do we have exemption from any of the pains and frustrations? To bring it down to practicalities, are our roofs exempt from leaks in heavy thunderstorms? (I ask because, while I was writing this, a cloudburst penetrated our roof's defences and totally ruined the bedroom and all its contents.)

When Paul comes to describe the state of the universe (in Romans 8:18–25), he recognizes that Christians are in a different position from others: 'We have the firstfruits of the Spirit.'

Groaning, frustrated

Then, however, Paul goes on to say that, even with the Holy Spirit, our experience is like this: We 'groan inwardly as we wait eagerly for our [final] adoption, the redemption of our bodies' (Romans 8:23) in glory. Not only that, but we cannot yet see our hope – with all the potential frustration that causes. So we need great patience to wait for it. And no wonder that in consequence we feel our weakness, not knowing what to pray for. No wonder that we need the Spirit to help us as he 'intercedes for the saints in accordance with God's will' (Romans 8:27).

We are in a very mixed world. The wheels, if not falling right off, are at least not running smoothly; the cogs do not mesh properly; grit has got into the works and friction is the result. The world is out of joint and we Christians are right in the middle of it, unexempt.

Mixed blessing

Earth is a mixed blessing and Christians tend to react to it in opposite ways. Some Christians have been so weighed down by the mixed nature of life here, so conscious of earth, that they have scarcely expected God to do anything. Groan and bear it until glory. Others have thought that we can have virtual heaven now – all our prayers granted, our ills removed, our needs met, life a magic carpet. Grin and claim it here and now.

Neither is true. God has not promised heaven on earth and is not yet giving all he can, and one day will, give. We have to wait in hope for the glory, this hope being a Christian distinctive. God gives touches of heaven, the firstfruits of the Spirit, the first instalment, the down payment, the guarantee. But the glory is for later.

Just listening

This is why the Christian life is never an easy ride. Some think that we are limiting God if we say, for example, that not all will be healed; on the contrary, we are simply listening to God. He has nowhere made universal promises to exempt every Christian from illness or suffering or redundancy or tough times generally. The only absolute, universal, apply-to-every-believer promises God has given are his gospel promises – that is, those that concern forgiveness and eternal life, not circumstances. What he has promised here is grace to help in time of need, his strength in our weakness.

One student had never appreciated this. She had seemed

a bright, happy, vivacious Christian in her Christian Union days, but when she graduated, she went into the spiritual wilderness. She came back to the Christian student camp two years later 'just to reassure myself that I made the right decision to walk away from God'. She had concluded that there was no way she could live up to 'this good Christian life'. As she said, 'After my struggles of these past two years, there is no way back to God for me.'

At the camp, they sang one song that moved her. She turned to her Christian friend and said: 'I like that song. It says that "God never promised sunshine without shadows". I thought that he had.' With tears in her eyes and true Christian realism now in her head, she came back to God.

Most of us know the story of Joni Eareckson Tada. When she was seventeen, a diving accident left her totally paralysed from the shoulders down. In a few seconds a young life of vigorous activity and independence became one of total helplessness and utter dependence.

She was landed with an agonizing struggle against quadriplegia and depression. Some urged her to seek healing. She struggled desperately for a meaning to life; she knew bitterness, confusion, violent questioning and tears. Her autobiography and other books tell of how she learned to trust, prove and honour God in her awful condition.

Suppose that another quadriplegic, or someone with Down's Syndrome, or a person with Alzheimer's disease were genuinely healed. That too would honour God. We do not need to pit one case against the other; God can do whatever pleases him. But few of us would doubt the greater effect for God that would come through the case of a Joni. For one thing, a healing, however amazing, is a one-off event; it cannot go on and on being news. Joni's case puts before us the grace of God every new day, a perpetual testimony to him. For another, Joni's story touches base with reality. This is often how things are (though, thankfully, not to that pitch of agony) in this world.

We have all come across believers who have not been healed. They may be told that it is due to their lack of faith. They castigate themselves for that: 'If only I had faith.' Their focus is on them and their 'failure' to trust God. That is a tragic situation for anyone, especially when God has made no universal promises of healing. Joni, by contrast, gives untold encouragement to all of us. Her focus is on God and that lifts us all.

Part of God's help comes from seeing his perspective on life. That is a brilliant help because it shows us what we can expect. Sufferings, frustrations and groanings will occur in life here. They do not show that God has abandoned us or left the throne of the universe. They do not mean that God has picked on us. He is not punishing us for our lack of faith. They are not occasions for surprise or blame or resentment. However hard we may find it to understand particular circumstances, we know that they are here by the will of the God who is in charge (Romans 8:20).

Yes, God is fully in charge. The fact that the universe is creaking on its hinges does not deny that it is God's Son who sustains all things by his powerful word (Hebrews 1:3). It is Christ who holds all things together and keeps them from descending into chaos (Colossians 1:17).

Total control

In the very chapter where Paul describes this groaning world he affirms that God works in all things for the good of those who love him (Romans 8:28). God is in such total control that, however we understand it, he is able to predestine and guarantee absolutely that those he calls will arrive in glory (Romans 8:29–30). God is sovereign so that nothing can separate his people from his love in Christ Jesus, not even demons or powers or death (Romans 8:38–39).

A mixed, malfunctioning world it may be, but it is not out of control. That is yet another reason why we can begin to see sense in life – the sense that comes from our Father's control and plan. To that plan he wants us to respond in three ways.

1. Contentment for ourselves

Contentment is an attitude distinctive of the Christian. It does not mean that we become resigned or passive. It is the attitude that says: 'Whatever happens, whatever I gain or lose here, whatever I experience of joy or pain, I have a hope in heaven and a Saviour in my life.' Paul's famous 'I can do everything through him who gives me strength' (Philippians 4:13) did not mean he could walk a tightrope across Niagara. It was in the context of having 'learned the secret of being content in any and every situation' (Philippians 4:12). There is even more reason for most of us to be content, when we see how few troubles we have compared to many Christians in other ages and parts of the world.

True contentment is independent of circumstances, which is why it is part of the Christian's freedom. Our happiness is not wrapped up in things or happenings (Luke 12:15), but in God. It is never easy; it has to be learned, as we take on more and more of God's perspective in life. It comes from realizing that the things that cannot be touched by circumstances are the things that matter and that last. They alone have weight and substance, whereas all our possessions, our stuff, are insubstantial and fading. So we need to learn contentment.

2. Growth in God

We also need to learn obedience, as Jesus did, through suffering (Hebrews 5:8). We need to keep on keeping on. When suffering or setbacks hit us, our first instinct is probably to complain and question: 'How could God let this happen to me? Where is his love now?' God, by contrast, wants us to turn suffering to advantage and to shape other questions in our minds: 'What should I be learning through this? How will God use his power, not to remove the problem, but to help me over and through it? What does obedience to God mean in this situation?'

I once asked those attending an international Christian conference to put down the three periods in their lives when they had learned most about God. The answers came out like this. Everyone confessed that one of those periods was a time of suffering: 95% said that two were; 90% said that all three were. We rejoice in the easy times (if we remember to give thanks); we learn and grow in the tough times. They develop us as human beings; they test our resources and resolve; they prove God's power in our weakness; they give us a perspective on what really matters. They show that God is greater than we thought, whether or not we fully understand all that he is doing at the time.

They turn our minds round; disappointments are not so much setbacks as opportunities with God. Failure can be the backdoor to success, as George Verwer says. We may certainly ask for deliverance and full restoration for ourselves or others, provided we are willing to accept God's will if he does not grant our request.

This radically Christian approach is underlined if we study the prayers of the New Testament. They are not generally at the level of circumstances or for material things. They are for things that matter and last, the ultimate issues of life. Jesus taught us to pray 'Deliver us from evil', not deliver us from discomfort. He prayed that we might be sanctified by the truth; that we might be with him and see his glory, not that we might have a sheltered life (John 17:17, 24).

Paul prayed that the Philippians' 'love may abound more and more in knowledge and depth of insight, so that you may be able to discern what is best and may be pure and blameless ...' (Philippians 1:9–10). He prayed that the Colossians might be filled 'with the knowledge of his will through all spiritual wisdom and understanding ... in order [to] live a life worthy of the Lord' (Colossians 1:9–12).

There is no thought in Jesus or Paul of getting bogged down in muttering about why the present world is so frustrating; their concerns rose above that to things that endured. That outlook changed the disciples' lives.

3. Compassion for others

When we feel that life is tough, our thoughts instinctively turn inward. Self-pity springs up. We focus on our problems and hardships. Our prayers tend to revolve around ourselves. The Christian reaction to being here, in a groaning world savaged by sin and evil, is to look outwards. Other-pity ousts self-pity. Awareness of the needs of others overtakes our own sense of need. This leads to Christian compassion in action, a heart concern directed to all forms of true human need.

Hebrews 13:16 says, 'Do not forget to do good and to share with others, for with such sacrifices God is pleased.' Doing good will involve sacrifice and cost; it never comes cheap, is never a token gesture. It takes something out of us. 'Let us do good to all people, especially to those who belong to the family of believers' – especially, but not exclusively to them (Galatians 6:10). 'Command them to do good, to be rich in good deeds, and to be generous and willing to share' (1 Timothy 6:18). 'Look after orphans and widows in their distress' (James 1:27). Or, as God said through both Moses and Jesus, 'Love your neighbour as yourself' (Leviticus 19:18; Matthew 22:39).

Involvement with others certainly does us good. It takes us out of ourselves and puts our circumstances in perspective; moreover, it lays up treasure for us 'as a firm foundation for the coming age, so that [we] may take hold of the life that is truly life' (1 Timothy 6:19). Put another way, we are never the losers when we give ourselves for others. The self-centred are those who lose out.

At a higher level, our prayer is that involvement for others will benefit them. And the scope for this is the whole world. If you have ever travelled to a country that does not have income levels near those of a western consumer society, you will know that you come back chastened and convicted over what we have and they don't. Many parts of the world lack basic necessities, though sometimes their people bear their deprivation with a cheerfulness and resilience unknown to those who focus on their 'relative deprivation' in relation to their neighbours' expensive new car.

This is why relief and development agencies have such a pull on the Christian's heart. This is why concerns for justice arise. This is why so many Christian students and young people give time to overseas or inner-city projects. This is all part of why God has put us here in this present evil world.

The scope of compassion covers the whole range of human needs, from food, water, medicine and shelter, to safety, education, justice and freedom from exploitation. Christians are rightly involved in all these spheres, even when (perhaps particularly when) needs and justice issues come into conflict with political, power or financial interests. It is often difficult for Christians to operate in such grey areas and to make wise judgments about when to speak out, what to say, who to work with, and so on. But the case for compassion is strong.

At the same time, the ultimate, basic need for all human beings is to be reconciled to God, to be forgiven and accepted through the death of Christ. We are all called to evangelism by the love of Christ that compels us to be his ambassadors (2 Corinthians 5:14,19–20) and by the Lord's Great Commission (Matthew 28:19–20). Evangelism is essentially concerned with calling people back to God. Its central message is about how people stand with God; that they are lost, condemned and guilty, needing the only Saviour. The words of Francis of Assisi are often quoted: 'Go and preach the good news to everyone. Use words if necessary.' Those who quote him are obviously making a point, but how can news be understood without words?

One of the dilemmas in helping others is that they may simply conclude that we are exceptionally nice and helpful people. What good news is that? No, evangelism inescapably involves the message of truth in words. 'Faith comes from hearing the message' (Romans 10:17), not from observing good deeds. Actions may well arouse people's interest and lead them to ask why we are bothering; but that is where explanation and the good news come in.

The relationship between evangelism and social concern is close and clear. The connection arises from the fact that God made us for time and for eternity, to start here and finish there. We were not made for this life only. God's concerns match his creation: for our life here on earth (and all our physical and other needs) and for our ultimate destiny (our salvation through Christ).

Social action is necessary for some people sometimes, but not for everyone always; evangelism is necessary for every human being everywhere. Social action looks at the question: How are people faring now? Evangelism takes up the question: How will they fare on the last day? Non-Christians can and do join in social action; only believers can engage in evangelism.

Compassionate action is not evangelism. It is not an alternative to evangelism or a substitute for it. Equally, the evangelistic imperative does not release us from present concerns. They are not in competition with each other. In the Bible it is not one or the other, but both. Human need is of an ultimate, eternal nature (needing the gospel) and of a present, temporal nature (needing relief, and so on). Both areas of need are genuine and make their challenge to us. Words without works are as empty as works without words. Words and works, Bibles and aid are both needed.

Compassion is a consequence of the gospel. Down the centuries and all over the world the Christian gospel has got into people and changed them, so that works of compassion have started to flow. Before Christianity seriously challenged and changed many countries' cultures, social concern – and even justice – were little known. The inward change that the gospel brings has had outward results: countless educational, social, medical, relief, development and other programmes, including political and legal action. Every person truly converted is at least a potential agent of change. This is why it is sad (and misguided) if ever evangelism is neglected for other legitimate concerns. To neglect that is, long term, to cut back the flow of people who will show practical concern.

Compassionate action is thus also a companion of the gospel, often a child of the gospel. It may pave the way for the gospel or follow its proclamation.

As we live in and look round the world, in its frustrations, pains, decay and groaning, we cannot but be concerned for others. When the gospel brings us to God, it changes our whole outlook and motivation so that we do get involved in this-worldly need.

No end in sight

We may agonize over why God does not instantly wind up this sin-weary world, abolish evil and bring in the new heavens and the new earth. (After all, he could.) All we can say is that he has not revealed the full answer to that. We have to trust his timing, plans and wisdom. He knows what he is doing. 'The Lord is not slow in keeping his promise' (2 Peter 3:9).

In the meantime, to see life in this world through God's eyes, as disclosed to us in the Bible, is a terrific basis to making sense of it all.

Attack in Kakuma

When Jan King took early retirement to go to work in Africa, it can't have been in her mind that she would witness the trauma of an armed raid by night ...

I sit alone in my little mud house in Kakuma Refugee Camp, with the terrible sounds of grief rising and falling around me. 'Why, Lord, why?' I ask myself.

A dozen of us were sitting in the compound. It had been a long hot day and we were relaxing in the cool of the evening. We had no lamp, there was no moon, so we sat with only the stars to give a little light. We were talking in small groups, one group singing quietly. It was a peaceful scene. Daniel, a young evangelist, was walking towards the gate of the compound when it burst open and a gunshot rang out. We heard a terrible cry from Daniel, 'Aheeh,' then silence. We all leapt to our feet and ran for our lives. I seized the hand of John Kuol, the young blind man, and we ran together. We were brought up short by a fence. Young John managed to wriggle under it and through the thick brushwood fence. I had thought that, at 64 years, my wriggling days were over! But I too was soon on my stomach, wriggling for dear life. I curled into a small ball in the thick dust and prayed – a wordless prayer, as I had never prayed before.

During our flight we had heard another shot, within the compound. It later transpired that the bullet had penetrated the side wall of one of the pastor's houses, but happily missed the pastor inside.

Two attackers

There seemed to be two attackers, one with a gun and one with a torch. It was impossible to tell if they were still in the compound. I was just aware of a presence, a menace in the dark. I remained motionless, shielding my head with my arms. After perhaps ten minutes another shot was heard, definitely outside the compound, towards the dry riverbed. Then again silence.

Some of our people began to come back, hesitantly. Some kind ladies helped me to my feet – the mixture of shock and arthritic knees had made it all but impossible to rise unaided. We stood together, in a small knot, holding each other. Very soon other people poured into the compound. An ambulance took Daniel away. Some of his relatives gave blood, then he was transferred to the hospital at Lokichoggio. The bullet had passed through his stomach and out at the back.

We were all dazed. Gradually we dispersed to our sleeping places. My compound was just seven mud huts in an unfenced area. I lay in the stifling heat, the only white person in that part of the camp, aware that my door was very insecure and that there were window openings on three sides. Sleep was impossible and I was still too bewildered to pray.

In the small hours of the morning a strong wind arose, straight towards my door. It brought clouds of dust and an occasional small stone. As each stone hit my metal door it gave a loud crack, causing me nearly to jump out of my skin.

Third shot

The night passed slowly – and then came the horrifying sounds of women wailing. The third shot had hit Pastor John Majok. The bullet entered his thigh and cut through an artery. He had tried to run away, but was bleeding freely. Then we saw in the sand the impression of his body, where he had pressed himself back towards a hedge. There he had bled to death. It was only in daylight that his body was found.

The Sudanese are a strong people. One of their strengths is their ability to gather together in times of sorrow, to support and console the bereaved. I felt privileged, as a *kawaja*, to be a small part of this process.

Eventually I got back to the security of my Nairobi home, finding it hard to believe that it really happened. But my jumbled emotions left me in no doubt. I realised that my initial question – Why Lord? – is not a question that we can put to God. If we try to penetrate God's intentions, we are sure to beat our heads on an impenetrable wall. The ways of God are not for us to know. We can only invite him into our situation and cry to him for comfort and for his sustaining power.

Although our voices may be trembling with pain, we can still declare: OUR GOD REIGNS.

From the *AIM International magazine*, by permission.

10
Talking to God

The Ethiopian Students Christian Fellowship is a striking illustration of the power of prayer. Its members regularly face opposition. This often comes from official religious quarters; sometimes Christians are banned from meeting on campus or in dormitories; sometimes new converts are expelled from their families, who disown them and strip them of anywhere to live and anything to live on. There is a huge cost to be counted by anyone who turns to Christ there.

The students react to this by prayer. If they cannot meet on university property, they go out into the bush. Wherever they can meet, they pray, casting their desperate situation on God; they ask not primarily for safety, but for many more students to turn to Christ. God answers. Now some 12% of the total number of students in tertiary education are in the evangelical student movement. Admittedly, overall student numbers are small compared to many other countries, but 12% … If only Christian students in other countries approached that percentage!

The story of the church down the ages is littered with remarkable answers to prayer – one reason why we should not be so locked into the present that we fail to recognize God in the past. The trouble is that prayer does not always 'work' like that. Maybe you have prayed for ten, twenty, thirty years for a relative and she is still resisting God. Perhaps you have had some affliction for a decade or more and still God has not removed it.

In addition to the personal agonies over prayer, we all meet the old vexed questions about how to understand prayer. Does prayer change God's mind? What bearing on answers does the amount of prayer have? If God is sovereign and working all things according to his own counsel, what is the point of praying? Won't he do what he is going to do anyway? How can we make sense of prayer? We all feel guilty that we don't pray more, but it doesn't help when we also feel mystified by the whole issue.

We need therefore to remember that God is infinite, while we are finite and fallible. We will not fully understand God in this life and, for that reason, need to be wary of pushing our logic too far. We may not be able to grasp how God's total control fits with him giving our prayers a place, but the Bible teaches both and we can take it that he sees how they fit together. The Bible is full of such truths: on the one hand, I repent and turn to Christ and I have to call on others to repent; on the other, 'No-one can come to me unless the Father who sent me draws him' (John 6:44). We will only make sense of God's grace, and the place of prayer within it, if we accept all that he has revealed. We must see that the fact that he said it is more crucial than whether we can figure it all out. If God were not in full control of the world, it would scarcely be worth praying to him; it is precisely because he is sovereign over everything that prayer makes sense – we can never ask what is beyond his power.

Then we need to look at Jesus. He clearly wanted to help us to make sense of prayer. We read about this chiefly in Matthew 6:9–13, where he comes to prayer from a fresh angle.

Expressing a relationship

Firstly, Jesus talks about the power of prayer to express a relationship. Prayer is not primarily about getting things done or even changing the world: it is a relationship, 'Our Father'. That is a sufficient justification for prayer, whether or not we ask for certain things. Indeed, Jesus knocks the bottom out of prayer as essentially asking by telling us that our Father knows all our needs before we come (Matthew 6:8). We can't tell him anything he doesn't know.

Christianity is essentially a relationship, a walk together, an ongoing conversation. Jesus stresses that his Father is different; he must have been aware of many bad fathers in his day, of many children who were turned off by the concept of a father because of their own bitter experience. This is 'Our Father in heaven', perfect, good, generous, kind, just. Life has no greater joy than to have this Father as ours.

'In heaven' also means he is powerful, in control, sovereign. He runs this world; all authority and rights are his. He is the Creator and Judge of all, but the Father only of those who have trusted Jesus. It is mind-blowing to be in this child-Father relationship with him. This is the heart of prayer. This relationship is for eternity and develops in many ways, not least as we talk. No-one can grow in a relationship without words; it is very sad to see colleagues or couples who have nothing to say to each other.

Jesus indicates that there will be times when we go into our room and close the door, to exclude distractions and talk with God (Matthew 6:6). We need to guard these. But, equally, conversation runs all through our lives. We are to be 'joyful always' and 'pray continually' (1 Thessalonians 5:16–17). We are to 'always keep on praying for all the saints' (Ephesians 6:18). Praying at all times cannot mean formal or withdrawn prayer; it must mean the ongoing, informal keeping company with God. There is no circumstance in which we cannot talk to God. If we are in a place or position where we know we cannot pray, we should get out fast.

Such a relationship means that God is our constant point of reference. In a good human friendship we often carry the other person in our minds and 'talk' to them: 'I wonder what he'd think of that. I wish she could share this …' We do that in our imaginations with others; we can do it in reality with God.

Jesus is telling us through 'Our Father' that Christianity is about grace and gratitude, security and joy. Prayer expresses that relationship. This emphasis directly helps our practice of prayer. Jesus does not want us to feel so guilty about our failures in prayer that we forget the relationship and fail to enjoy it. We know from experience that talking, listening, sharing, openness, doing things together enhance any relationship; and it is the same between us and God. Prayer is not only to be at specific times, but all through the texture of life in company with God. And not only privately, but also with others.

Establishing a purpose

Secondly, Jesus shows us the power of prayer to establish a purpose. His three phrases ('your name', 'your kingdom' and 'your will') set out a perspective for our praying. As our prayers incorporate his ideas, we are taken along in his direction. We can see this if we note what he is not saying.

He is not saying that we are to promote our name or image, though we all have an instinct to do so. The magazines and the media push questions at us all the time: What will people think of me? What about my looks, my clothing, my hair, my weight, my intelligence? Is my image right? An industry lives off the beauty myth, but Jesus is diverting us away from such self-concerns. Our life's purpose is to make a good name for God. As I pray 'Hallowed be your name', I should be concerned about whether people get the right impression of God from watching me.

He is not saying that we are to run our own lives. We all want to be in charge, to have everything under control, to be on top of life, calling the shots. But the prayer is: 'Your kingly control come into my life, my world.' Our prayer purpose is to see others coming increasingly out of rebellion and under his rule. We want the world and ourselves to submit to God. He is the king; our prayer is that that becomes apparent and accepted.

Jesus is not saying that prayer is a mechanism to get our will done, though we can easily try to turn it into that. We may draw up our list of wants, call them needs, pray for them and expect to receive them. That is not Jesus' mind. True prayer is seeking that God's will be done. This prayer of Jesus stands our natural desires on their head. Prayer certainly includes asking, but this means that we should ask God what to ask for. Those are the prayers he delights to answer.

If we genuinely pray these prayers, how can we work them out? We can know God's will from the Bible – what attitudes and actions please God. The focus is more on what we are and become than on what we may do. For example, Peter wrote: 'His divine power has given us everything we need for life and godliness. ... For this very reason, make every effort to add to your faith goodness ... and knowledge ... self-control ... perseverance ... godliness ... mutual affection ... love' (2 Peter 1:3–7). We are in no doubt about God's will for our character and conduct.

We can also seek God's will in particular circumstances: career choices, whether to pursue yet more job applications, what to do about a problem in church, how to help that other family, and so on. The prayer reminds us that our purpose in life is to honour God's name, submit to his kingship and follow his will.

Changing our character

Thirdly, Jesus reminds us of the power of prayer to change our character. Jesus teaches us to pray four things here (Matthew 6:11–13): give, forgive, lead and deliver. In telling us what to pray for, he tells us a lot about ourselves and how he is working to change us.

When we pray, 'Give us today our daily bread', we are recognizing that we have needs. We depend on God every day. The bakery shelves in Tesco's and Sainsbury's mask but do not override our dependence on God. Every single day we are vulnerable. Every single day we would crumple and die if God did not preserve and supply us. We are weak and frail. God has found ways throughout history of cutting down to size those who get too big for their dependency boots. This phrase changes us as we truly pray it.

When we pray, 'Forgive us', we are feeling our sinfulness and proneness to stray. We keep going wrong. We keep doing things, saying things which need forgiveness. We don't love God as we should, we follow him only erratically. Our temper, impatience, anger, laziness or passions get the better of us. We can get so complacent before God that we even half-wonder: 'What do I need to be forgiven for today?' This prayer changes us as we pray it, as we confess our sins, as we face our reluctance to forgive others.

When we pray, 'Lead us not into temptation', we are not entertaining the idea that God would lead us into evil; rather, that we walk knowingly into temptation, we fall into the devil's old traps, we get ourselves into risky situations. We are like that. This prayer is a signal to us about what we are like, so that we may be careful. It works away to change us.

Finally, when we ask, 'Deliver us from evil' (or the evil one), we are remembering the opposition and our weakness to handle it. We are easily led into evil and need to be reminded of that.

When we pray such prayers, what is happening? It is not that we are changing God's mind, but rather that he is changing ours. This is not a version of positive thinking. It is just that we cannot repeatedly pray from the heart, 'Give, forgive, lead, deliver', without developing different attitudes to the people or circumstances involved. Such prayers, sincerely and thoughtfully prayed, will be shifting us from self-reliance, hypocrisy, self-will and evil thoughts to what God wants us to be. He already knows all about us: 'Your Father knows what you need before you ask him' (Matthew 6:8). We are not informing God of anything he doesn't know, but he is moving in us to introduce the changes he wants.

In any human context a relationship has the power to change the participants. They come to see things from the other's point of view, they absorb the other's values and they change. How much more in our relationship with God. The more we converse with God along the lines of Jesus' prayer, the more his ways will rub off on us. We will gradually change, as his will is done in us as well as in the world through our prayers.

In this way we become part of the answer to our prayers. This is the power of prayer. This is part of the way in which God's programme goes forward in the world.

Prayer has its mysteries, but these aspects make sense from Jesus. We can accept God's purposes for his name, his kingship and his will – and seek to conform to them.

Impulsive, frustrated, doubting

James became the editor of a distinguished newspaper at the age of only twenty-two, renaming the paper *The Sheffield Iris* and working on it for another thirty-one years. He carried it through a period of great national tension over war with France and agitation for parliamentary reform. He was twice arrested and imprisoned for allegedly publishing seditious material. He knew many years of deep depression.

His father had been a preacher and had wanted James to follow the same calling. He sent him to a particular school to train him for such work. James wanted none of this. Then, when he was twelve, his parents left him and his two younger brothers and went to the West Indies as missionaries, where they died a few years later.

At school, James was warned, exhorted and threatened until it was decided to 'put him out to business' as a baker's assistant at Mirfield, near Wakefield. He ran away one Sunday morning while his boss was at chapel. He repented of being impulsive, but a year later took himself off to London, hoping to be published as a poet. That dream faded as publishers rejected him. When he went back north, he became assistant on the Sheffield paper – and took over when the editor emigrated.

James could not entirely throw off his family's beliefs, but felt acutely the frustration both of failed ambitions and of what he called 'religious horrors'. He spoke of his 'most dreadful apostasy of spirit'. He often felt 'tossed to and fro on a sea of doubts and perplexities'. His life only began to turn round when he was thirty-one, when, in search of spiritual peace, he attended a Methodist Chapel and a 'class meeting' (a home group) in a member's house. Even after that he knew periods when he lacked full assurance of being accepted by God.

In later life he wrote: 'I cast him away – but he did not cast me away. Goodness and mercy have followed me all my days ...'

An impulsive rebel, a long-time doubter, a failed poet and a busy newspaper editor, James did not seem qualified to write about prayer. It was James Montgomery, however, who wrote the following words (and many others, like 'Angels from the realms of glory'). He lived from 1771 to 1854.

Prayer is the soul's supreme desire
expressed in thought or word;
the burning of a hidden fire,
a longing for the Lord.

Prayer is the simplest sound we teach
when children learn God's name;
and yet it is the noblest speech
that human lips can frame.

Prayer is the secret battleground
where victories are won;
by prayer the will of God is found
and work for him begun.

Prayer is the Christian's vital breath,
the Christian's native air;
our watchword at the gates of death,
we enter heaven with prayer.

Prayer is the church's glorious song,
our task and joy supreme;
we name our Lord in every tongue,
and praise is all our theme.

Jesus, by whom we come to God,
the true and living way,
the humble path of prayer you trod,
Lord, teach us how to pray.

This version © by Jubilate Hymns.

11
Finding guidance

Paul, a man to put our spirituality to shame, set about finding and following God's will in a trusting, almost matter-of-fact way. He did not get into contortions about whether his motives were 100% pure or whether he had read circumstances correctly.

He and other New Testament Christians seem to have had an optimism and an opportunism that seldom figure in our approach to guidance. They made more sense of it than we often do: why? We do all the right things: pray, wait on God, look into his Word, consult with others, look at needs, and so on. Yet guidance often remains mystical, even mysterious. We look for 'a sense of peace' in a decision over which house to buy; when we have that sense, we may feel we don't need that dry-rot check. And guess what we discover six months later? We thought we had found guidance over which church to join, but after a while other factors come to light.

Our mental tangles often come because we fail to think rightly about the will of God. We know that the rule of God governs everything, as he 'works out everything in conformity with the purpose of his will' (Ephesians 1:11). This is the sovereign will of God. He has revealed its broad sweep and its grand design, but often its detailed outworking remains hidden until later on.

We also know what we might call the moral will of God: what attitudes and behaviour please him. 'Be holy, because I am holy' (1 Peter 1:16). His will is for us to become upright, loving, generous, good. We are in no doubt that he is in total control of the world and intending us to be righteous – he is supremely concerned for what we are, our character as well as our conduct.

Within his overall plan for the universe and in line with his moral will, God is concerned for every aspect of the life of every one of his children. This is initially and notably evident in where, when and how we come to Christ. This plan includes all our circumstances, jobs, health, moves, and so on. God knows everything about us from before birth to after death.

The problems arise when we make the wrong deductions from all this. We often infer that it is our business before God to try to uncover the secret individual plan for our lives, so that we can be 'in the centre of his will'. Our role, we feel, is to ask of every possibility: Is that God's will or not? Am I meant to take this job in banking or that one in computing? Is John/Rachel the right one for me to marry? Is this the right flat to buy or does God have another one for me? The two university courses seem about the same: so is Warwick God's will, or is it Southampton?

Those are well-motivated questions: we want to do God's will. Then, however, other questions arise: If I choose banking, will I be wrong? If I opt for someone other than John, will I have missed God's best? If I elect to take a place at Southampton, will I have stepped outside the centre of God's will?

The questions get hotter if things do not work out neatly. Now I'm in banking, am I condemned to be off-centre with God for the rest of my life? Wouldn't life have been good with John? Did I just choose Southampton for my own reasons, did I really care about God's will at all? Now I'm paying the consequences. Why did he make it so hard to know? Why couldn't he just have told me whom to marry, what job to take?

The truth is that God has our whole lives in his control, from the day we were born to the moment we die. The question is: what does he want us to conclude from that great truth? The answer is a positive and a negative. The deduction we *should* make is that we should and can trust him. He is greater than all our circumstances, our doubts and our mistakes. His loving and sovereign control is in ceaseless operation every moment. The deduction we *should not* make is that he wants us ferreting around for the one job, house, partner or course that alone is 'in the centre of his will'. God does not mean us to be trying to decode the messages conveyed by a mixture of prayer + Bible + counsel + circumstances + feelings + intuition. That is a fallacy that can lead to deep frustration. These are helpful pointers, but not absolute rules.

The will of God that we should be seeking, as the Bible repeatedly insists, is to do with what we are, more than where we are. The Bible gives us a *freedom* that has three elements. One is that we can be quite clear about the moral will of God. God is more concerned with what we are as people than what we do or where we do it. Honesty, integrity, love, concern, diligence, contentment; in short, godly living is set out for us all through the Bible. We don't have to 'find guidance' in that sphere, for God has shown us what pleases him. It may be hard to be honest in a corrupt firm; but that we should be honest is not in doubt. It may be hard not to envy materialistic neighbours; but that we should be content with what we have is not in doubt either. There is a great freedom under God in this way; lots of decisions that vex others are lifted from Christians. This is why we can talk of God, 'whose service is perfect freedom', echoing John 8:31–32.

The second element of biblical freedom is that we can trust God: he is already constantly guiding his children. We don't have to ask him to guide us, starting now; we can rejoice that our whole life has been under his active direction, since even before we were born. 'The LORD is my shepherd … he leads me … he restores my soul … he guides me' (Psalm 23:1–3) – all in the present tense. The fact that 'he restores' us clearly implies that we slip and fall; and for such sinning we need to confess and seek forgiveness from God. Sin matters because it always grieves him. We have no licence to displease him, but his guidance is in motion all the time, through our ups and downs. We can trust him; nothing that turns up can surprise him. No circumstance comes as a setback to him. Everything is under control. This yields terrific confidence to our hearts, a confidence that is immensely strengthened when we have the gift of hindsight and can see how God did lead us through circumstances that, at the time, seemed impossible or overwhelming.

The third element is that God wants us to go on acting as 'humans being restored'. He wants us to form judgments and take decisions. We are not at liberty to decide not to be honest: that is a 'given'. But where God has not spoken one way or another, we are free and called to decide.

This means that many decisions are not matters of right or wrong, but of wisdom or folly. It is not right to catch the 08.17 train and wrong to go for the 08.40; but it may be wiser to get the earlier one and leave yourself unrushed at your interview. It is not right to serve God in Africa and wrong to serve him in Afghanistan. It is not wrong to marry John and right to marry Bill (unless one is a non-Christian); but it may be crazy to marry John (who, though cool, is essentially uncaring) and wise to marry Bill (who does not have the same image, but is very creative and considerate). The Bible has its 'wisdom books' to emphasize this very point: in the crucial decisions of life, be wise, decide wisely.

When I was doing a management course, I came across one guru who won my vote. He said that there was only one rule to follow: 'Use your best judgment at all times.' If we understand 'best judgment' to be based on the masses of wisdom in the Bible, then that is thoroughly biblical advice. That is the Christian's freedom. It helps us at those points when guidance seems a problem and we don't know what to do – or think or pray. There is a vital principle here that we need to apply: at such points, go back to what we *do* know.

When we don't know what to think, God calls us to

think what we know to think – all the basic truths about his character and ways. When we don't know what to pray, God calls us to pray what we know to pray – for his will to be done in us and in others.

When we don't know what to do, God calls us to do what we do know to do. When we don't know what to do in the 'guidance' sphere (about a job or a move, for example), we still know what we should do in terms of discipleship – to go on living out the Bible, growing in grace and seeking wisdom from God. Often it is as we keep up these means of grace that guidance becomes clear.

The New Testament underlines this in many incidents. When the council met in Jerusalem to settle the vexed question of what to require of Gentile converts, they were guided in such ways as these: 'It is *my judgment*, therefore, that …' (Acts 15:19); 'The apostles and elders … *decided to choose* …' (Acts 15:22); 'We all *agreed to choose* some men …' (Acts 15:25); 'It *seemed good* to the Holy Spirit and to us …' (Acts 15:28). We might think that there is nothing very spiritual-sounding about deciding, choosing or forming judgments. On the contrary, that is God's way for 'humans being restored'.

Paul in prison wrote: '*I think it is necessary* to send back to you Epaphroditus' (Philippians 2:25). On another occasion he wrote: 'If it *seems advisable* for me to go also' (1 Corinthians 16:4). He '*did not think it wise*' to take John Mark (Acts 15:38).

There is no hint in all these instances of seeking special revelation, messages from the Lord, pictures, visions or words, though clearly God could give Paul a vision (Acts 16:9). Obviously, they prayed and sought God. But what was their general practice? It was to use their minds, weigh things up, seek wisdom and take decisions. Even Paul did not claim: 'God told me not to go with John Mark' or 'The Spirit revealed who to send.' They decided. That was spiritual activity, not unspiritual. It was the freedom God gave them – and us.

God's purpose in granting this freedom is not so much to get us into the 'right house' in the 'right job' in the 'right place'. It is to help us to grow up into Christ. We would never grow if we could press the prayer button on the divine computer and have a printout of the right answer for every problem. We might *do* the right things, but we'd hardly be developed or stretched.

Children and adults learn and grow by the decisions they take. Often we learn from our misjudgments; they make us stop and think, confess and seek better judgment. The management course I attended highlighted one interesting finding. People who had always been top of the class at school, who had consistently got 'A' grades, who had got firsts at university and maybe had been a star in the school and university sports teams were unlikely to be very good in management. Why? Because they had never known failure, they were reluctant to take risks, and so ended up achieving little. They kept the wheels going, little more. Others who had ploughed the odd exam, had wasted the year after school or had been dropped (unjustly, of course) from the first eleven – they had made mistakes, learned from them and gone on. They had grown as people.

The Bible is full of believers who blew it at one time or another. Abraham and Sarah were singularly unwise in not trusting God to keep his promise. Abraham brought himself a heap of trouble by going down to Egypt in the famine and deceiving Pharaoh about Sarah (Genesis 12:10ff.).

David sinned grievously on more than one occasion (2 Samuel 11). Peter not only denied Jesus three times, but acted foolishly in giving in to those who wanted a gospel of 'Jesus plus Jewish practices' (Galatians 2:11ff.).

These very characters also at other times showed great love and wisdom. Abraham allowed Lot to choose the land; David loved and cared for Jonathan; Peter accepted the Gentile, Cornelius. They all grew into great people of God, despite (or through?) their mistakes.

It is similar in the Christian life. Taking decisions may sound scary, but is a great way to grow, provided we are willing to review what we do and continually ask God for wisdom (James 1:5). And we have this freedom under the constant guidance of the Lord, our Shepherd.

In Acts we also read that Paul had been 'kept by the Holy Spirit from preaching the word in the province of Asia ... they tried to enter Bithynia, but the Spirit of Jesus would not allow them to.' But 'during the night Paul had a vision of a man of Macedonia standing and begging him, "Come over to Macedonia and help us" ' (Acts 16:6–9). God is free to give that spectacular kind of guidance; he does not promise it, but he can and may give it. Paul received it and heeded it, but did not bank on it every time.

The same can happen today. I know a Christian in Oslo who, totally out of character for him, once felt that God was calling him to get on a train to Trondheim, several hours further north. He was completely baffled, but convinced that he should go. Hours later the train arrived, passengers got out and still he did not have a clue as to why he'd come. Eventually, the platform cleared, apart from one other man. The Christian thought he'd better talk to him. It transpired that the man was intending to throw himself under the next train. God was in that guidance, though nothing like it has happened to my friend since.

Is there any *formula*, then, for making wise and godly decisions? On what are we to base our 'best judgment'? The Bible's thrust can be summed up under four directives:

First, we need to *aim*: we need to clear our motives, so that we are seeking God's kingship in our lives (Matthew 6:33). We need to settle this, not to keep going over it. To be in two minds about whether we want God's way or our own is a recipe for instability. It is difficult to steer an unstable craft. There must be no question of whether we want God's will: we *do* want it. And no question of whether we think his will good: it *is*. Though our feelings may wobble, we must never give in to materialistic or coveting motives or to seeking status or image; rather we are to be single-minded for him, remembering what we owe to Jesus and his self-sacrifice.

Second, we need to *ask*. We should not under-pray and neglect to seek wisdom, but neither should we over-pray – that is when our praying becomes introspection and shuts us up to probing our own feelings. Rather, we can commit the particular matter to God, and leave it with him; this is what Peter means when he says, 'Cast all your anxiety on him', so that he carries it, not you or I (1 Peter 5:7). We can ask God to shape our thoughts and values, so that (as in those quotes from the Acts) we too can say: 'It is my judgment that ...'

Third, we will want to *assess*, to weigh up all the pros and cons. This means seeking to be objective, asking the advice of others, taking a long-term view, relating the decision to what we already know of God's grace and gifts. Caution is sometimes called for, lest we simply ask the advice of those who will say what we want to hear. As we assess things like this, we can expect the peace of Christ to act as the umpire in our hearts and to confirm one way or another.

Finally, we come to the point where we must *act*. When we've prayed and weighed, we must decide. We need not fear this moment; indeed, such times can turn out to be terrific experiences with God, going into the unknown, but seeking to live as the human he is restoring, with him knowing the unknown and going with us. Life has few adventures left for many today, so why not enjoy this one? Any good parents would much prefer a child who made a few mistakes in attempting something to one who sat and did nothing. That's how babies learn to walk. And, like a good Father, he will back you up as his child, even if he may redirect you on occasion.

Once we have tried to reach a wise decision, we must then trust God to work it out and rest in his grace and power. This is sometimes far from easy. We can get quite nervous about whether a decision was wise. At such points we may need to review that choice, but basically we need to go forward, knowing that God is well able to get us back on track if he needs to.

This brings us back to our Father. He has given us his absolutes, so that we have the freedom that comes from knowing right from wrong and good from evil. He has given us the freedom to make decisions on issues that don't involve those absolutes. And he has shown us the guidelines for such decisions. All this is backed up by his character and grace. When David said 'he leads', he also said 'he restores' (Psalm 23:1–3). God knows when we need to be picked up. He restores us when we fall or fail, grow weak or weary. He knows what we are like and still the next verb is 'he guides me'. This way, guidance is just as much from God (indeed, more so), but much less mysterious and elusive.

'Who are wise and understanding among you? Let them show it by their good life, by deeds done in the humility that comes from wisdom' (James 3:13).

Making mistakes

A father sometimes forgets Paul's command: 'Do not exasperate your children' (Ephesians 6:4). He doesn't mean to – he loves his family, but it happens. He wants to exercise discipline in a self-controlled way, but finds himself saying things that, though factually true about the children, are selective, unfair and wounding. When his children blurt out their response, he puts them in their place for their impudence and lack of respect.

As soon as he gets on his own, he knows that he's blown it again: What is he to do? 'Well, they were in the wrong – *again* – and I can't let that sort of behaviour pass', he replies. 'They've got to learn!' But all they learn from such exchanges is to keep out of Dad's way whenever possible. He feels uneasy, but can't bring himself to admit his mistakes or undo the injustice to them, lest it undermine their 'respect' for him.

Anyone who admits mistakes can greatly encourage others to go forward. His attitude will prompt people to think: 'He doesn't always get it right, but God uses him.

I don't always get it right, so maybe …' Few things are more dangerous or discouraging than 'infallible' people, whether parents, partners or pastors. To recognize mistakes is the only way on and up.

Our fear of mistakes regularly stops us from attempting new things for God. We don't try any new initiative for fear that we'll end up with egg on our faces. So we keep to the same old ruts, unadventurous, unimaginative, unadvancing, unbelieving.

Those who are going out to others, in the spirit of the Great Commission, may be the most likely to make mistakes. After all, 'out there' is uncharted territory. But what if the venture does fail? Many will be their critics, but at least they attempted something for God. At least they learned some new lessons. At least they put their talent to work. And they find that their heavenly Father picks them up, sets them on their feet and backs up their next venture.

Some define a mistake as a 'learning opportunity'. Under God, mistakes can be turned to advantage. At the very least, we can make the best of a bad job. Admitting a mistake carries this great benefit: it confesses that we care more for God, for truth and for others than we do for our own image. And that is a huge step forward for any of us.

12
Meeting with others

How do you feel when you roll out of bed on a Sunday morning? That is a pretty good index of what you actually think of church, your church.

You may leap out of bed with great enthusiasm: 'Hey, it's Sunday again everybody! Let's be getting ready. God really met with us last week; I'm sure he will again.' Or you may want to pull the covers back over your head. 'Church last week was so dreary, boring, irrelevant, out of touch (delete any that don't apply) that it is not worth going again.' Or your church may be average, somewhere in the middle.

Being severely realistic, churches have both inspired people and deflated them. They have motivated some, demotivated others. They have been warm, welcoming communities, and they have been cold and formal. Some have been pillars of the truth, others have thrown truth out. It is sometimes not easy in practice to see the value of the church, which is why we need to go back to the New Testament.

Realism and experience

Before we do that, however, and at the risk of sabotaging the whole chapter, realism demands that we recognize a serious problem at this point. The theory of church is one thing; the experience of it can be quite another.

This was vividly illustrated for me when I visited a group of Christian students in a Russian university while the Communists were still in power. They had to meet secretly and certainly valued whatever fellowship they could get. When I asked them about the local churches, they looked crestfallen: 'The Baptists just want to get you baptised, the Pentecostals to get you filled and the Orthodox – well, they don't even talk to you.'

At the time when they needed the church most, it failed them. Sadly, though less dramatically, that is the experience of many who find 'church culture' very hard to handle.

Mixed reactions

Church culture can take many forms and prompt a variety of responses. It can, for example, lead some Christians to feel welcome and out of place at the same time. They sense that they are more welcome the more they conform or keep quiet. To some, the church is a 'control zone', squeezing them into its sub-cultural mould.

Some who developed a large circle of non-Christian friends before their conversion now feel that they could never bring their church and their non-Christian friends together. Some of their church friends basically live in the world of the church and would not understand the others. They would not know how to strike up any conversation or rapport. These 'Christians in the middle' are in limbo between the two cultures, sometimes feeling that the non-Christians are more honest and real than the Christians.

Giving up

As I write this, I know of a bunch of converted students who have given up on what is generally regarded as a thriving church. They love God and now meet together for Bible study and mutual encouragement. They know that it is wrong to neglect the church and do not hold themselves blameless. Their church, however, felt oppressive to them, simplistic in its patterns and responses, over-demanding of their time and loyalty, and repetitive and boring.

Some try to solve their dilemma by going to one church in the morning for the worship and a quite different one in the evening for the teaching. Still others, in similar settings, have given up church altogether, even after serving it for years. They felt they 'needed a break' or that the church did not deliver what it kept promising.

Not always living

Some of the reasons for these reactions are clearly at fault. Sometimes they spring from an attitude to church that basically asks, 'What's in it for me?' But not always. Many genuinely long for their churches to honour God, make Christ known and build up the people. Whatever the reasons (and describing them is not excusing them), this scene is tragic in a generation that is so fragmented and needing to 'belong'. It is tragic too that some Christians with lots of unbelieving friends feel that the church is so alienating.

It is simplistic to say that we need to get back to the New Testament church. Ironically, the churches that such people are leaving are often those that claim to be most in line with the New Testament.

As with many other aspects of the Christian life in a fallen world, we need to keep working at it – in prayer, with patience and encouragement, by hard work and involvement. What follows here will try to show a little of what God means the church to be and what we should be aiming for. We certainly need to keep reviewing our church life in the light of what the Bible says. And maybe, as we work this out, our churches will end up with fewer meetings to attend and more occasions of people actually meeting people.

Three ingredients

In essence, all that any local congregation needs is light, love and life. The light that comes from the Word of God, the love that took Jesus to his cross and the life that flows from the Holy Spirit. Just three basic ingredients for a community of God's people; that is not much to ask. Yet sometimes churches claim to have life while neglecting light; or they claim the light but overlook love.

We will not, however, make sense of the church by starting where we have just started, with the problems. We think of church and immediately bring to mind our (imperfect) local manifestations. We need to start in God's mind, with his perspective on the church, and then work through to the problems. 'Once you were not a people', Peter wrote (1 Peter 2:10) – you were out on your own, you did not belong to a lasting community, before God you were a lost individual – 'but now you are the people of God.' You have entered his community, you belong there. That is your home, they are your people, you are now one with others. This is part of the mercy we have received from God (1 Peter 2:10), that he has incorporated you. You'll never walk alone any more.

God's brilliant idea

The church, for all the failings of its human members, is a brilliant idea of God. It does not choose its own members, like a club or party; God does – a chosen people. (We would probably not choose half of those God does.)

It is not a tin-pot society of cranks, but a royal priesthood. It is not a quaint back-street sect, but a nation called and separated to live distinctively for God. It is not a group who assert their rights to run things their way, but a people belonging to God. It does not exist for its own happiness and benefit or for its leaders, but to 'declare the praises of him who called you out of darkness into his wonderful light' (1 Peter 2:9).

Seen together

This novel kind of body must meet. Obviously. If the world is to see that its members love each other, they must be seen together. 'Declaring praises' is a plural activity, so 'let us not give up meeting together' (Hebrews 10:25). The early church met 'on the first day of every week' (1 Corinthians 16:2). Paul taught 'publicly and from house to house' (Acts 20:20). A church met in the house of Aquila and Priscilla (Romans 16:5).

So why did the church meet then and why should the church meet now? What is the purpose of a church assembling? In particular, what should it do when it is together? Presumably something that it cannot do when it is apart. The church is still the people of God when its members are scattered around the town or country during the working week – at work, at home, in business, with the children, putting in the overtime, waiting in the job queue. During the week they can sing praise to God, read his Word, pray, give and serve. During the week they can worship, not in the narrow sense of having a band leading them in singing songs, but in the whole-life sense of worshipping God in all they do. One church I visited in Ulster caught this idea neatly, with a little sign in the vestibule that could only be read on the way out: 'Worship begins now'.

Seven days a week

Undoubtedly we ascribe worth to God when we come together to sing praise to his name. There is a buzz and a thrill then that we do not so easily recapture on our own. But there is no doubt that worship, which equally means service, is what we are meant to do seven days a week, twenty-four hours a day. Unintentionally to confine worship to two hours out of 168 a week is to skew life away from God's pattern. Our reasonable worship/service means our bodies being living sacrifices all the time we are in them and our minds being renewed all the time they have not atrophied (Romans 12:1–2).

The New Testament never calls us to come together to worship. (If that sounds surprising, check it out.) Old Testament believers were called to go up to worship because 'God is in his temple'. New Testament believers can worship anywhere. Jesus' conversation with the Samaritan woman makes that clear; worship now is not limited to specific places, but is to be in spirit and in truth wherever we are (John 4:23). We need to get our words to match the Bible's theology here, or we will have trouble making sense of church. 'Worship' is one of the most misapplied words in Christian circles.

Why to meet?

So why are we to meet? And what are we to do when we get there? We are to 'Let the word of Christ dwell in [us] richly' as God's chosen people; and we are to 'teach and admonish one another ... as you sing psalms, hymns and spiritual songs ...' (Colossians 3:16). We are to 'speak to one another with psalms ... Sing and make music in your heart to the Lord' (Ephesians 5:19). It is vital to have music and accompaniment that serve the words and convey their sense, rather than music that primarily creates a mood.

We can obviously sing praise direct to God, as many psalms do. Such praise is 'vertical', upwards to God. The singing that Paul mentions is 'to teach, admonish and speak to one another'. It has a horizontal aim, outwards and across to others. It is to do others good by conveying and expressing good teaching and wisdom – we sing such songs with our eyes towards other believers rather than shut or upwards to God. If all this is to happen, any music must carry and clarify the words and the words must have truth as their content.

In other words, we meet for each other, not only for God. Hebrews 10:24–25 is very clear about this: meeting together is related to considering how we may spur each other on to love and good deeds. It is so that we may 'encourage one another – and all the more as you see the Day approaching'. This is a radical angle. We must not think of 'praising God' as the superior activity and 'encouraging one another' as more mundane. It pleases God greatly to see his church built up and this is a chief way in which he does that. It is a pity that there is not a more exciting or user-friendly word than 'edification'. 'Worship' versus 'edification' sounds like no contest! But building his people up is in the forefront of God's mind when we meet. We are called to a life of worship or service all the time, but the main ways of edifying each other happen when we meet.

The main New Testament passage reminding us to meet for the Lord's Supper or communion is in the first letter to the Corinthians and is in a context where Paul is rebuking the Christians for their self-centred individualism. 'As you eat, each of you goes ahead without waiting for anybody else ... do you despise the church of God and humiliate those who have nothing?' (1 Corinthians 11:21–22). Rather, Paul urges, 'when you come together ... wait for each other ...' (1 Corinthians 11:33). The Lord's Supper is to remember Jesus and his death, but it is to be celebrated together, with a sense of corporate participation.

Much is sometimes made of 'praise' or 'the high praise of God'. So-called 'warfare praise' is loosely drawn from a speculative reading of Psalm 149:6–9. High praises are believed to move the powers of darkness, even to tear down Satan's strongholds (2 Corinthians 10:3–6). All sorts of questions arise about this approach. Does the venue affect the efficacy of the praise? Do numbers increase its power? It is probably a slur on the Old Testament to say that these are rather Old Testament ideas. In Psalm 149 it is more likely that the 'double-edged sword' that affects God's enemies could be taken as the Word of God, rather than as praise. When Paul writes of 'divine power to demolish strongholds' (2 Corinthians 10:4), he makes not the slightest reference to praise. As we saw earlier, the power to demolish strongholds is truth. That is why 'We demolish *arguments* and every *pretension* that sets itself up against the *knowledge* of God, and we take captive every *thought* to make it obedient to Christ' (2 Corinthians 10:5).

Central focus

The devil is the father of lies; God's weapon against him is truth revealed in Christ and in his Word. In consequence, we will have much more effect against the enemy if our churches open and apply the truth than if they major only on 'praise'. The adversary is quite happy for us to sing our hearts out, if we are not bringing God's Word to bear in our lives and world. Again, the Word is central – the living Word, Jesus; and the written but contemporary word, the Bible.

That is why the Word of God is so crucial. It is that word that 'can build you up and give you an inheritance among all those who are sanctified' (Acts 20:32), not just a nice feeling with this week's singing. It is the God-breathed Scripture that makes people wise for salvation and then equips Christians for every good work (2 Timothy 3:15–16). A church without the teaching of the Bible is a shell only. A church which can let a meeting pass regularly without opening the Bible and taking it seriously is like a car about to run out of fuel and leave its passengers stranded (2 Timothy 4:2).

Ministry to each other

With the Word of God central, the members all have a ministry to each other. The bottom line of what Paul teaches about life and gifts in the church, the basic test of what is acceptable, is 'that the church may be edified' (1 Corinthians 14:5). If 'others are not edified' by some practice (however good or innocent, like 'giving thanks well enough'), then drop it. Edification is the chief purpose of the church; exercise of insights or gifts is secondary. Tongue-speakers may edify themselves, but only prophesying (defined in 1 Corinthians 14:3 as 'strengthening, encouragement and comfort', which must be based on God's revealed truth) edifies the church. Hence Paul's further exhortation to the Roman believers: 'Let us therefore make every effort to do what leads to peace and to mutual edification' (Romans 14:19).

This 'mutual upbuilding' has a very practical bearing as we go to church. It encourages us to think not 'What will church do for me?', but 'How can I encourage someone else?' Most of us are liable to judge church by whether we like it; Paul encourages us to view church as the sphere where we can strengthen others. Why not ask God next Sunday morning: 'Lord, give me someone today who needs strength or encouragement. Help me to do them good.' That is right in line with God's idea of why we meet.

Schism by songs

Such an approach would go a long way to cutting through the jungle of worship-style preferences. Too much organ, too loud a band, too short a flow of songs, too little/much repetition. We separate on personal likes and dislikes, forgetting that we go to encourage others and to welcome and celebrate variety. Some churches are locked into one music style: the result is that we have what a friend of mine called 'schism by the song book (or the OHP)'. There is almost infinite musical variety available: Bach and blues, soft rock and classical songs, choruses and hymns, barber-shop and jazz, solos and groups, paraphrase and poetry, guitars and orchestra,

Welsh and English and German and Scottish ... to say nothing of Country and Western!

Why do we not use at least some more styles or musical genres? It would take a bit of planning, but the outcome could be terrific as people emerged from their musical cubicles and enjoyed the variety with which God has flavoured his church.

Adapting to others

We do not come to church to satisfy our individual preferences, but to adapt to others (mutual submission, Ephesians 5:21) for the overall good. Church is not for me to 'make my communion', as I shut out all the others around me; it is not the place where I shut my eyes to the point of just doing my thing with God. It is a together event. It involves meeting, greeting, enquiring, opening the Bible, encouraging, talking, praying with others.

It is bizarre that both ends of the worship spectrum tend to become individualistic. The very conservative worshipper comes in, bows his head, prays and retires into his own thoughts, with barely a nod to anyone. The very upbeat worshipper gets going in the flow of songs, hands raised, eyes shut, in another world with God, blotting others out. Where is the meeting in that? Moreover, we don't have to 'put from our minds all the thoughts and worries of the week' and become a 90–minute recluse. We don't have to stay silent when we are coming into 'the house of God', because it isn't the 'house of God' – each member and each member's home is a 'house of God'. The early church met in houses (Romans 16:5) and you don't enter a home and lapse into self-enclosed silence. You meet. You talk. You share. False ideas of worship have a lot to answer for. Sometimes we are too spiritual.

If we came intending to strengthen, encourage, comfort and build up others, the church would make a lot more sense and many more would have their spiritual vision and vigour restored. It would say to everyone: 'Others care about you. You matter to us.'

All this can happen only if we come together and come consistently, reliably. That will happen only if we settle in our minds that we will be there. If we raise, every week, the question of whether to go, we will never contribute or benefit. Encouragement is unlikely to be given or received if we appear only spasmodically. Absence or erratic attend-ance will deprive us of meeting around the Lord's Table and being reminded of our debt to the cross of Christ. It is great to be committed to our particular circle of friends or our home or fellowship group, but that can be little more than an expression of self-interest: we go to what we like, what gives us a buzz.

God looks for rather more than that. Since his church is an all-age, all-types, all-temperaments family, he wants our commitment to the whole church. Only when we move from our comfort and preference zones will we con-tribute to his church and be built up ourselves. It was the whole church that was devoted to the apostles' teaching, fellowship, breaking of bread and prayers (Acts 2:42). It was on that basis that outsiders were filled with awe.

Appropriate response

This is the only appropriate response to the fact that God chose the church's members. If he chose them, he wants us to relate to them. We may have to go beyond our own boredom thresholds or tolerance limits, but we in turn will appreciate such thoughtfulness when our needs grow or we get old. A head teacher recently told a parents' evening: 'When you and your son or daughter open the school report, remember before you speak that it is he/she who will be choosing your old people's home only a few years from now.'

These are some leading features of God's church. Like everything else on earth, it is not and never will be perfect here. But, by God's Spirit 'the whole body ... grows and builds itself up in love, as each part does its work' (Ephesians 4:16).

The gospel of God produces people who are leaving self-centredness behind and becoming God-concerned and other-concerned. God wants us to run that gospel effect on into our church lives. Then we will begin to get the picture.

Vertical and horizontal

Ministry exercised in love amongst the people of God is a sign of the Spirit's transforming power already at work in those who believe. Ministry exercised for the building up of the body of Christ is a significant way of worshipping and glorifying God.

... If the focus of the meeting is on the edification of the church, this should enable God's people individually to engage with him afresh and to offer themselves to him in the way that he requires and himself makes possible through the Holy Spirit. Thus, the 'vertical' and the 'horizontal' dimensions of what takes place should not be artificially separated. One part of the meeting cannot be 'the worship time' (*e.g.* praying and praise) and another part 'the edification time' (*e.g.* preaching), since Paul's teaching encourages us to view the same activities from both points of view.

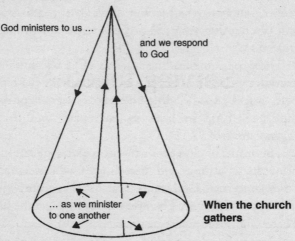

God ministers to us ...

and we respond to God

... as we minister to one another

When the church gathers

The God-directed ministry of prayer or praise and the notion of edification are intimately linked in the New Testament (*e.g.* Colossians 3:16; Ephesians 5:19). Even 'psalms and hymns and spiritual songs' (RSV), which are expressions of faith and thankfulness to God, are to be considered simultaneously as the means of teaching and admonishing one another. This does not mean that prayer or praise is a means to an end, namely edification. We worship God because of who he is and because of his grace towards us. Participating in the edification of the church, however, is an important expression of our devotion and service to God.

David Peterson, *Engaging with God* (Apollos, 1992), pp. 220–221.

13
Serving together

Those who meet together, to teach and be taught, to give and receive encouragement, are also involved in serving together. We are all called to work with others in and beyond the local church. God has much that he wants us to do. The sense of a shared vision and a common calling is a powerful incentive to be active for God. We are all prepared to work hard together when we know that the project is worthwhile and feel that everyone is pulling their weight (and in the same direction). A 'community project' can be exhilarating as well as exacting.

This is why leaders in the church, and in other areas of God's work, are so crucial. They can have a powerful effect on our lives. Good leaders can free and fire up others to be active for God and to be rich in good deeds (1 Timothy 6:18). Poor or perverse leaders, on the other hand, can exploit people and leave them discouraged and disillusioned.

Some, of course, are called to formal leadership

positions, but we all have some relationship to leaders in the church or other areas of Christian work. How can we make sense of leadership within the church? What is it meant to do and where is it meant to lead? What is its nature and what are its limits? How can we tell a good leader (or a bad)? This is not a great issue in any fellowship when things are going well. But if the leaders 'get it wrong', it is a very hot potato. Leaders can help our Christian lives to make sense or they can make them seem pointless.

Naturally, the Bible has much to teach on leadership. For a start, it shows the place of leaders in God's mind and plan. This is why it encourages us 'to respect those who work hard among you, who are over you in the Lord and who admonish you. Hold them in the highest regard ...' (1 Thessalonians 5:12).

Being an overseer is a noble task, since it involves taking care of God's church (1 Timothy 3:1, 5). An overseer is 'entrusted with God's work', so that he can 'encourage others by sound doctrine and refute those who oppose it' (Titus 1:7, 9).

This is why the letter to the Hebrews (13:17) says: 'Obey your leaders and submit to their authority.' Clearly this is not blind submission. Even Peter, the apostle, was at least once 'clearly in the wrong' and 'not acting in line with the truth of the gospel' (Galatians 2:11, 14). This is not a charter for authoritarian leadership; leaders may call people to follow them only in what is in line with the truth. But, that said, they should have our respect, affection and prayers. They are not infallible, they are involved in hard work and they need all the wisdom and grace we can ask for them.

We are not going to look here at what leadership system, positions or titles a church should have. Our focus is on two basic issues: what a good leader is; and what a good leader does.

What a good leader is

A leader's character is crucial. This is the indispensable basis for all good leadership. If this is not right, no candidate for leadership should be considered. Jesus' character was the foundation of all he did. Although he was tempted just as we are, he was without sin; holy, blameless and pure (Hebrews 4:15; 7:26). Paul's main passages on qualifications for leaders major on character: above reproach, self-controlled, hospitable, not violent but gentle, not quarrelsome, not a lover of money, not conceited, having nothing against them, blameless, not overbearing, not quick-tempered, not given to much wine, and so on (1 Timothy 3:1–13; Titus 1:6–10).

Character considerations come first, even before gifts. A leader may have all the gifts in the world, but if grace and humility are lacking, if character is flawed, that leader will in the end undermine the church. We should never be taken in by gifts alone, though they may dazzle. Sadly, the greater the gifts, the stronger the temptation to exploit them. Great giftedness can go along with three things a good leader should *not* be.

No autocrat

Leaders may be pulled towards an over-directive style, as if they are at the top of a little hierarchy. In the worst cases they mistake authoritarian for authoritative. They often operate by inducing guilt. They are issuers of directives, of words and rules. They seem on a power trip. They are heavy with people and defensive when criticized. They are like the 'rulers of the Gentiles [who] lord it over [others], and ... exercise authority' (Mark 10:42). The higher the title people claim for themselves, the greater this danger. Leaders can become very status-conscious.

That never strengthens anyone, leading rather to external conformity and a fear of failing the leader. That stifles questions, suppresses others' gifts and puts the collective foot on the brake. We need discernment to spot the difference between manipulation and leadership.

No follower

By contrast, other leaders follow majority opinion. They resemble politicians who say whatever will get votes. They want to please everyone, to have everybody on their side. They are all the time trying to second-guess what people are thinking, so that they can be in line. They have no courage or conviction to do the unpopular thing when it is right. They are pathetic and will never put strength into anyone. We can never discuss an issue with such people, because they are interested in their position, not truth.

No priest

Priests do not exist only in Catholic or Orthodox circles. Priesthood is growing in other circles too, not in name but in practice. A priest stands between God and the people; he is a go-between, an intermediary. God cannot speak to the people except through the priest; the people cannot approach God apart from the priest. A priest is necessary to make the connection between us and God.

Some churches exalt the preachers, as though we can know the truth only through them. A friend abroad came across three churches: one called itself simply 'the church

164

of God', another 'the true church of God', a third 'the only true church of God'. We can give the impression that we are the last, all others being wrong. If so, we put ourselves between people and God.

Other churches exalt 'the worship leader', the one who can move us through the flow of worship and tell us where the Spirit is working. In most churches, happily, a worship leader (though misnamed) is simply an unassuming music leader for the songs or hymns, not putting on any airs and graces. (If that is the case, why not call him or her a *music* leader?) But if anyone is becoming indispensable to connect God and people, a new priesthood is arising.

He is a servant

With society's models of leadership setting the trends, and when we all share human pride, it is not easy to find good Christian leaders. Christian leadership sometimes struggles to buck the secular trends and be different, but different it must be.

The true leader is a servant, a fellow-worker, a player-coach. Leadership is probably not the best word to convey the Bible's idea, since it tends to imply 'power' and public image emphases, rather than serving ones. Facilitators and mentors are the current terms, and they have much truth. Godly leaders have authority not because of office, but because their character and work elicit respect. People know that they serve. They are in office because they have already been exercising leadership and showing wisdom. No-one becomes a leader on appointment; true leaders are leading others, even when they are not recognized or in a formal leadership position. Ultimately leaders are those who have followers.

Such leaders are approachable, out and about, not locked away behind desks or pulpits. They work together. All the earlier examples were at least of pairs (such as Paul and Barnabas) and the New Testament churches had teams of overseers and deacons (Philippians 1:1). They do not coerce, they persuade, knowing, as one management guru said, that 'intelligent organizations have to be run by persuasion and by consent'; and surely the church is an intelligent organization?

What a good leader does

We cannot do better than observe the best leaders of the early church in the Acts. First of all, they gave themselves to spreading the gospel, and all biblical leadership has that end in view, whether directly or indirectly. The gospel must be in every leader's heart. We look at this in the last chapter.

Secondly, they devoted themselves to the Word of God. This is why they had to be able to teach, to preach the Word, to hold firmly to the trustworthy message, to encourage by sound (health-promoting) doctrine, and to teach what is in accord with sound doctrine (1 Timothy 3:2; 4:2; Titus 1:9; 2:1).

Thirdly, they applied themselves to bringing this Word to the people, the churches. Paul and Barnabas returned, '... *strengthening* the disciples and *encouraging* them to remain true to the faith' (Acts 14:22); 'Judas and Silas ... said much to *encourage* and *strengthen* the believers' (Acts 15:32); 'Paul and Barnabas ... taught and preached the word of the Lord' (Acts 15:35); Paul and Timothy travelled '... so the churches were *strengthened* in the faith and grew daily in numbers' (Acts 16:4–5); 'Paul set out from there ... *strengthening* all the disciples' (Acts 18:23);

'When the uproar had ended, Paul sent for the disciples and, after *encouraging* them, said good-bye ... He travelled through that area, speaking many words of *encouragement* to the people' (Acts 20:1–2).

Bound to the Word

Their input, strength and encouragement were closely bound to the Word of God, the faith. They certainly gave human sympathy, to 'comfort those in any trouble' (2 Corinthians 1:4). They shared 'not only the gospel of God, but our lives as well ... [working] night and day' (1 Thessalonians 2:8–9). But above all they strengthened people by the Word of God, they encouraged people in *the* faith. No leadership is authentically Christian that does not aim to strengthen and encourage.

The work of a Christian leader, at whatever level and in whatever sphere, is at root to seek to 'let the Word of God do its work'. That Word speaks to all people and situations; a true leader brings Scripture to each situation, to let the Word do its work there. This can be in a large church or one-to-one, with a non-Christian student or a dying friend. We need to pray for and appoint leaders with this approach.

A godly leader, therefore, promotes growth. When people are nourished and encouraged, they change. There is no way a good leader can avoid change. The status quo is never a way forward. A key element for any leader, therefore, is handling change. And we need to be willing to support change that is biblically based. If good change is rejected or bad change embraced, we will find life ceasing to make sense.

Guiding change

A leader therefore has to guide change: to prepare for it, to usher it in persuasively, to pick up and tend to those who may feel left behind. A leader must understand change and discern how and when and at what pace it comes in. Things will not be the same in us or our church or our organization this time next year, we will be stronger or weaker. Good leaders try to prepare us for that.

No surprises

A good leader will be sensitive in introducing change, knowing that it is not so much change as surprise that will frighten some. If change is jumped on a church or a Christian Union, fear of the unknown will be uppermost in all minds. Unannounced, unprepared-for change is a threat – understandably.

Few things are more unsettling in a church or Christian group than what Charles Handy calls 'group-think'. This 'comes about when well-meaning people become too close and cohesive to challenge assumptions, to check out facts, to explore new options or to risk too much argument. It is often more important to agree together than to get it right' (*The Age of Unreason*, Arrow Books, 1990).

A good leader will not look to appoint only conformists who never rock the boat or question decisions or make mistakes. He will not want people who simply maintain the system. He will be very keen on openness and listening – what has been called 'naïve listening', when a person listens, not to get the answers he wants, but to hear the answers that come. Listening tells people that they matter, a crucial element in a good leader. When he listens, he will get questions and be able to ask questions. He will welcome questions that ask 'Why?' about what is already being done and 'Why not?' of any new idea.

Reframing the question

He should particularly value questions that reframe the problem. If, for example, we are reviewing our church or Christian Union, we might ask: What are we actually doing in our prayer times, our evangelism, our adherence to sound doctrine? Are we actually praying, actually reaching others, actually promoting truth? Or are we meeting out of habit, going through the motions or defending our own orthodoxy?

Imparting vision

Good leaders work for and with change as they set about strengthening and encouraging others. They do this particularly by the way they shape and share their vision. A biblical vision for the church will focus the work of everyone and help us to see where we are heading and how we fit in. It is crucial that our vision be understandable. Some vision statements have been bland and simplistic, but there is value in trying to put down our vision in a single sentence which we and everybody can carry in our minds. Some Christian Unions have encapsulated their basic vision as 'gospel and growth' or 'mission and maturity', for example. Even if we don't operate only out of the single sentence, it is a good exercise for all of us to try to capture our vision in a brief statement. How would you express your church's vision?

We may be able to put our vision in flowing words of Scripture, but often these remain pious generalizations. No-one would know if we had achieved them or not. We need a vision that is totally biblical, and that can be expressed in clear, current English. If we cannot express it clearly, we probably haven't grasped it clearly. Leaders and led need to be involved in this together.

Delegating, handing on

As Paul did with the younger Timothy, so good leaders seek to impart their vision and bring others on, to give them openings and responsibility, to encourage them to have a go for God. They share and they delegate. 'I have no greater joy than to hear that my children are walking in the truth' (3 John 4). Leaders take pleasure in others' faithfulness and success. They encourage us through our failures, knowing that getting it wrong is often part of getting it right.

True leaders let the Word of God shape their vision and agenda. Their concern is not to get position, but to accept responsibility; not to be up front, but to be whole-hearted; not to be seen, but to be serving. We all need those who strengthen and encourage us. When we have such leaders – in church, home groups, Christian Unions or any other area of Christian work – we should be profoundly thankful. Then we will be able to get on unitedly with serving God and being up and doing and for him. The sense of being in on God's community project can make his work a joy.

First things first

If a church (or Christian Union) sees the importance of Bible truth, how should it shape its programme? All Scripture is breathed out by God, so clearly we should note all the truths it teaches. But there are so many; where do we start? The Bible suggests its own truth priorities, its own ranking. Some truths are 'of first importance' (1 Corinthians 15:3–4); others, equally true, are not. The 'first' truths start with Christ, the cross and the resurrection 'according to the Scriptures'.

Jesus had priorities; when everyone was looking for him for healings, he said, 'Let us go ... so that I can preach' (Mark 1:32–39). The evangelistic addresses in Acts all focus on the core truths of the gospel and on applying them to various groups of hearers. Acts 20 shows the truths on which Paul focused for Christians. Though Christ commanded baptism, Paul said: 'Christ did not send me to baptise, but to preach the gospel' (1 Corinthians 1:17). He gave priority to 'five intelligible words' over 'ten thousand words in a tongue' (1 Corinthians 14:19).

Building others up in the faith was more vital than individuals insisting on their gifts, just as character (the fruit of the Spirit) and love are prerequisites for usefulness, whatever a person's gifts (1 Corinthians 14:6; Galatians 5:22–23; 1 Corinthians 13).

Paul gave priority to accepting one another, 'as Christ accepted you', over settling a dispute about what to eat and what days to celebrate (Romans 14:1–15:7). He made the cross alone infinitely more crucial than other issues.

The Bible gives us plenty of suggestions as to what is supremely important and urges us to get to grips with and express our unity in those truths. Christians can live with differences on secondary issues, providing everyone keeps them as secondary issues and does not turn them into tests of acceptability.

Historically, the church has highlighted the core truths in its creeds and confessions of faith. Today that good tradition or 'handing on' is expressed in various ways, not least in a doctrinal basis. My IVP paperback, *Ultimate Realities*, opens up UCCF's doctrinal basis and suggests how the central truths can find helpful expression in teaching and evangelism programmes.

14
Work as worship

I can remember quite clearly when I had my first 'Christian' thought about work. I had not long graduated and in the first few years after leaving university our batch of ex-Christian Union members circulated a news and prayer letter.

As I read one of these, I was amazed to find a pattern through every entry: 90% of news was about Christian or church activity; only 10% was on work. A typical entry read: 'Am now on the eldership/PCC with large responsibility for … I teach an adult Bible Class … help with the Youth Fellowship … serve on the committee of a missionary society … lead a teenagers' camp in the summer … we now have two children and I work for ICI'.

So unimportant

Was work so unimportant that it merited only four words? Something had got badly out of proportion. The theology conveyed by entry after entry was that work was a necessary evil and that the focus of life was in the 'spiritual' realm. Life was divided into two spheres, the spiritual being obviously superior to the secular. Mark Greene, who has written an excellent book on work (*Thank God it's Monday*, Scripture Union, 1994), discovered that 50% of evangelicals have never, in all their church lives, heard a sermon on work. We seem to think that missionaries are entitled to send out prayer letters, but not managers or motor agents. (Don't we all need prayer? Managers and motor agents probably have just as many pressures and opportunities to speak for Christ as the average missionary.)

False distinction

This division of life into the sacred and the secular immediately raises the question: 'Well, what's the point of my work – other than to earn enough to be able to give time and money to Christian activity? There is little sense to my working life (the majority of my time), if it has no particular significance for God.'

So how to make sense of work? Again, we need to go back to the Bible. When God created man and woman, it was 'to let them rule over' the sea, the air, the earth and all creatures; in other words, to work (Genesis 1:26). They were to 'be fruitful ... fill the earth and subdue it' (Genesis 1:28). They were to work the land. Their work was in the physical, material and mental realms; the spiritual was not mentioned. After they rebelled, they were still to work, though then it would be with pain and sweat.

Jesus worked: 'Isn't this the carpenter's son?' (Matthew 13:55). Paul worked, maybe all his life, as a tentmaker like Aquila and Priscilla (Acts 18:3). Work was part of God's original purpose and he has not gone back on his plan.

Underlying this is the fact that God does not recognize, indeed he flatly rejects, the sacred/secular distinction. Nowhere is this clearer than in Paul's instructions to slaves in Colossians 3:22–24. There is hardly a more menial, low-grade, unsanctified job than being a slave – so if Paul encouraged them, we can all take heart in our work.

How to work

First, he told them how to do their work, the attitudes to have: 'obey your earthly masters in everything ... not only when their eye is on you and to win their favour, but with sincerity of heart and reverence for the Lord' (Colossians 3:22). Something as spiritual as conscious reverence for the Lord had a bearing on their working lives. 'Whatever you do, work at it with all your heart, as working for the Lord, not for human masters' (Colossians 3:23). Work was important enough to call for whole-hearted involvement and the same attitude as in anything done directly for Christ.

Second, Paul told them what would follow: 'you know that you will receive an inheritance from the Lord as a reward' (Colossians 3:24). Their 'secular' work would have a direct connection to their inheritance in heaven. How they did it here would affect their reward there. That is a phenomenal significance for work. We could imagine that leading someone to Christ or bearing unjust suffering with grace or standing firm for God under pressure could affect us in heaven. But work can too. It is up there with those other and obviously 'spiritual' activities. Work has eternal ramifications.

Third, Paul told them what they were doing in their

work. 'It is the Lord Christ you are serving' (Colossians 3:24). Being a slave is Christian service in the highest sense. They could do that apparently secular job in a spiritual way and in that be serving King Jesus.

When Paul finished his section on slaves, masters and work, he went straight in to 'Devote yourselves to prayer, being watchful and thankful. And pray for us ... Be wise in the way you act towards outsiders' (Colossians 4:2–5). He moves to 'spiritual' factors such as prayer, but not as though he is moving into a different realm. Work and prayer are both part of our life, one sphere. In this sense, the world is one. It is all God's world. Everything that we do in it can be done for God.

This distinction is not between activities that are intrinsically worldly and others that are exclusively spiritual. It is between whether we do things for God or for ourselves. Slaves might have worked only when their masters were watching: they would not then have been serving Christ. Christian leaders can do their work to promote themselves; if they do, they are not serving Christ either.

It all matters

The Bible's conclusion, then, is that all our work matters to God and all of it can be seen as serving Christ. It matters partly for what it is: Paul obviously wanted the slaves to do their actual jobs well. It matters, perhaps even more, for the way we do it – our attitudes, cheerfulness, thoroughness, honesty, application, and so on.

When, therefore, those of us who have jobs roll out of bed on a Monday morning, this is what we can say as we rush for the train: 'My worship starts here, divine service is about begin.' Sure, it may not feel like that – the dreary stack of undealt-with orders, the colleague who staggers in after a dubious weekend, the boss who never listens. Paul would say: all the more opportunity to do your work differently: 'Let your conversation be always full of grace, seasoned with salt, so that you may know how to answer everyone' (Colossians 4:6).

On spiritual service

In the light of all this, several things follow. For example, you don't need to put yourself down before God or in your own mind because you are not a missionary, though if he wants you to be one, you should be one. You don't need to think your work unimportant to God. You don't need to compartmentalize life: if you have to work late and so miss the church prayer meeting, you are still on spiritual service. Do it for him, while remembering the counter-danger that you can become immersed in work and let it take over your life. Above all, you are out there for God where people are: that is a fact of unimagined significance for the cause of God. Moreover, you do not need to put yourself down if you are out of work and seeking to be usefully active.

Think how we do much of our church evangelism. Special events, family and guest services, barbecues – all events which involve inviting non-Christians out of their safety zones and on to our patch. They don't know how to behave when they come, or what to expect. No wonder they are a little apprehensive and the atmosphere half-false, half-strained.

Rubbing shoulders

By contrast, all the working members of the church, not

to mention those who have contacts in the community, are rubbing shoulders every day with the very people we would all strain to get to church. They work with them for 60% of their waking hours. The non-Christians can see them in all kinds of situations: under pressure, hassled, rushed, busy, slack. They can see their attitudes to ethical issues: stealing the firm's time, and so on. They can have meals with them, do lunch-time shopping with them, in short, be thoroughly in their lives. That ought, in the normal course of life, to offer opportunities to talk. Conversations don't need to be directly Christian to begin with. As one of my colleagues says, the basic problem is not how to start *Christian* conversation, but how to start *serious* conversation. If anything serious does come up, it is but a short step into something Christian.

Many news headlines have serious elements behind them, which can be raised. Many individual lives have serious problems or tensions, which may, in due time, be aired with a sympathetic Christian. All these factors and openings are also part of God's plan for human work (Colossians 4:2–6).

Tremendous pressures

As we have hinted, work can present huge problems, but that is only to be expected in a 'groaning world'. Some people face tremendous pressure to sell themselves to their company and to make work their life; weekends and family considerations take a back seat, or else 'you are not committed'. Others face moral dilemmas, either with the formal policy of their company or bank or else with the accumulation of dishonesties in practice. Some have to contend with the one-upmanship, finding it hard not to be sucked into the surrounding back-biting. Some do not want to have to keep up with the others, as they display their salary level in the latest suits, jewellery and cars. Others find it hard to see how they matter as one insignificant cog in a vast multi-national.

Alternative testimonies

These are points where the church should help. If there are few sermons about work, there ought to be more. But failing that, meeting other people at church ought itself to help those in work. Back to edification again. It would be great if some of the mutual encouragement could involve some honest sharing of what it is like at work: what we like, what we dread, our dilemmas ... A church could get a business person or a car mechanic or a secretary to give a testimony about life at work, provided it is honestly done and not made too 'spiritual'. That could encourage discussion and prayer. A testimony that simply told how tough it was would be quite a refreshing change!

Christians need help on many work-related issues. What is proper ambition for a Christian? How do we evaluate careerism? What do we do when we get a promotion and all our colleagues have instantly bought bigger houses as status symbols? How do we work out our giving if our salary keeps rising? Does our standard of living have to keep going up? How do we handle making someone redundant? How do we cope with redundancy or unemployment?

Churches need to give thought to their unemployed, remembering that work in the Bible is not defined as society commonly does today; as simply an activity that carries a wage or salary. Certainly the Bible recognizes a connection between work and income; it says that, if anyone *will* not work (that is, refuses to work), he should not eat (2 Thessalonians 3:10); and that people should provide for their relatives (1 Timothy 5:8). But it never downgrades unpaid work as non-work. Activity can be useful, indeed indispensable and highly valuable, even if it is not financially rewarded (look at all the work that keeps homes and families going). Unemployment can be desperately hard and depressing, as experience has shown me; but even then it is in principle possible to seek to be usefully active in ways that honour God and help others. The church needs to be alert to its members in this position.

Christians also need help on how to relate church and work. When does a church demand too much of its working members, in the way of evening or weekend commitments? How is family meant to fit in between church and work?

Many of these problems are a hang-over from the old, discredited distinction between sacred and secular. If we can kill that off in our minds, as the Bible does, then we will know that our work does make sense within God's plans. Then we will be able to do it with gratitude and understanding and see its place within God's total scheme.

Mobile

Upwardly

Peter joined the firm straight from school. He'd got good 'A' levels and was taken onto the training scheme as a potential high-flyer. Everyone made a fuss of him and painted rosy pictures of future (not-too-distant) promotion.

At first all went well. Peter enjoyed learning the new skills, was a good listener and a quick learner. He had an easy way with people and was popular with both his peers and his seniors. He'd never been earning before, so was more than happy with his better-than-average income.

Then, the training period ended and routine grind began. Not only began, but went on and on. Promotion seemed no nearer than on day one.

After work each day, he'd meet his old school friends and compare notes (notes in the pocket or the bank). Most of them had been promoted or got rises. Hadn't he? Well, no, not yet. What sort of firm did he work for, then? What was he going to get out of it? Why not change? Look what's in it for you ...

His firm had an outstanding record in looking after its employees, but Peter began to think other pastures were greener. An offer came, through a friend; it brought more money in the short term. 'You'd be a fool not to take it,' they said. 'But I said I'd give three years to my company,' he replied. 'Well, please yourself, but I know what any sensible guy would do – the trouble is, your firm doesn't appreciate you. Don't you want to better yourself?'

Downwardly

What was in it for him? What sense could it make for him to leave heaven for earth, glory for degradation, the bonds of the Trinity for the betrayal of Judas?

What sense did it make when he came down? He came to his own, but his own did not receive him. Crowds heard him gladly, until they pulled back. The disciples followed, until they forsook him and fled. No home. Nowhere to lay his head. What was in it for him?

They used him, exploited his healing power and love, took the bread he gave and executed him. He gave himself and they gave him nothing.

What if he had 'moved on' before the crux, concluding that there was nothing but hassle and hurt? What if he had allowed himself to be governed by people's rejection of his teaching and his gifts? Where would we have been then?

Thankfully, he did not go by 'What's in it for me?' He did not come to be served, to get, to have, to possess, to dominate, to be noticed; 'the Son of Man ... came to serve, and to give his life as a ransom for many' (Mark 10:45).

15
The Christian mind

'You're a Christian, aren't you? What do you think of the lottery … of the advertising industry … of abortion … of that film last night?'

Such questions can come unannounced and pressing. Sometimes our friends will accept that we don't have all the answers on our tongue. But other opportunities may not be there tomorrow; we may not have time to look out a Christian answer and come back to them. It is probably then or never. And if never, then we've blown it again and let God down. What do we say, as we teeter on the brink of a serious discussion? We know we can't pass it off with 'Well, everyone is entitled to their own view' or 'It's all a matter of personal choice.' Christianity has more conviction to it than that.

Struggling to find a lead

What we are struggling to find at such moments of opportunity is a Christian mind, a biblical outlook that will give us a lead into each area of life. If we only knew how Christianity approached such issues, we might be able at least to explain Christianity, even if we were still not fully able to defend it.

Moreover, it is not only that it would be good to have some guidelines to answer non-Christians; it would be great before God to know how to think Christianly about that novel, this music, our career, the advertising industry, the role of TV, teenage violence, third-world debt ... or even competitiveness and the place of sport in life. These are not matters only for self-conscious intellectuals, but for all thoughtful believers. We know that the Christian life is much more than personal piety. We need to discover its truth basis as well. We need to know (because this is how God made it) that it has an intellectual undergirding.

How then do we develop a Christian mind? We can start by reminding ourselves that everyone, however well or poorly educated, has a 'mind' about life, whatever they believe about God. That 'mind' covers their aims, values and beliefs, the things that matter to them. That mind is based on certain assumptions about ultimate issues. The assumptions may be hidden; the person may be unaware of them. But underlying all approaches to life are assumptions that relate to such questions as whether there is a God, what is he like, how we know right and wrong, or what happens after death.

Those presuppositions or ideas result in all of us putting down 'markers' in our minds, the fixed points which we refer to when judgments are made. For example, ideas of 'personal happiness' could give such markers, so that decisions are made on ethical, financial, sexual or other matters by how they affect personal happiness and fulfilment. And ideas about 'happiness' are obviously affected by whether or not there is a God, a judgment and an afterlife.

Ideas have a very powerful role in everyone's lives. Everybody acts on ideas. Jill devotes herself to research because she believes passionately in its ability to change society. John gets drunk every Friday because he thinks it is more fun than staying sober. Every action comes out of an idea, every idea out of a worldview or a 'mind'.

Other minds at work

It is easy to see how other 'minds' work. A Communist mind is now largely defunct, but in its heyday it formed its judgments on the basis of certain markers: the class struggle, the proletariat, 'from each according to ability, to each according to need', the flaws of capitalism and, of course, atheism. A Communist formed his view of the cold war or imperialism or work or sex by reference to such markers.

A materialistic mind has its markers too: this world is all there is. The present moment is it, prosperity is the way to fulfilment, happiness is our right, and there is no God. Countless people have formed their goals and values with such markers.

The same 'markers approach' is found in every religion or thought-system ever invented. In this sense we all have a mind, a set of beliefs and values, a worldview. The question is: is ours Christian? A Christian mind is often noticeable by its absence today. If everyone has a 'mind', how do we seek a Christian one and what are its markers or guide-posts?

That there is a Christian mind is not in doubt. It is not the consensus of Christians, but comes from the personal and rational God who has revealed himself. His is the mind behind the universe and the Bible. That one mind gives unity to all that he has said and done. Every part of the Bible conveys part of his thinking, and we need to take an overview of the Bible to get his overall drift.

The Bible begins with Genesis and ends with Revelation; it opens with God creating the world and closes with him bringing it to his conclusion. It gives us what we may call a horizontal or historical axis. If we have a question about why things are as they are, about the purpose and nature of things, then creation will have light to shed on it. If we have a question that touches destiny, goals, the end or fulfilment, then the climax of all things will have a bearing on it.

If we look at the Bible more closely, the horizontal axis includes many facts and truths, such as human rebellion, the fall; God's providence in history; the coming, dying and rising of Jesus Christ; the sending of the Spirit; the formation of the church; the world-wide spread of the gospel; and ultimately the return of the Lord Jesus Christ and final judgment.

The Bible also reveals what we could call a vertical or spiritual axis; supreme over all is the Creator, distinct from all his creatures, the only God. Beneath him is the creation, with human beings in God's image over that creation. In the depths, as it were, are the powers of darkness, with Satan at their head.

Taking these two axes together, they give us markers or reference points, the distinguishing features of a Christian mind. Out of the infinite range of truths that the Holy Spirit has given us in the Bible some major markers stand out as follows:

1. God
2. Creation
3. The fall
4. Jesus Christ
5. The climax

A Christian mind takes all these into account, seeking the Spirit's help to understand them from the Bible. We can move towards framing a Christian mind as we start to investigate these markers.

1. God

The Christian sees everything in the light of God. He exists, he is there, he has spoken. Everything rests on the fact of God. We are committed to a view of life which has a supernatural orientation. We have an 'other-worldly' mind, not at all in the sense of denying this world, but of affirming that this world is not all there is – that there is an invisible world, a world to come that is more real even than this. We also have an 'other-standards' mind, since God is holy. He is the arbiter of right and wrong, not public opinion or personal preference. He is the Lord and giver of life and therefore the one who alone has rights over life and death.

He brought creation into being and has the final say in how it should be run. He established its 'hierarchy', with humans as the pinnacle of creation, over the animals and all else created. And he has revealed himself in the Bible, giving his mind on the whole of life.

We can read Wayne Gruden's *Systematic Theology* (IVP, 1994) or similar books to discover more of the attributes of God. But taking God as our first marker, a Christian mind will always ask: how or where does God come into this? What is his view? What has he said? What are the consequences of leaving him out?

If, for example, we ask about a Christian mind on the lottery, the fact of God will immediately contrast with its totally this-worldly, materialistic preoccupation. Our mind will be infinitely sad at so many people so affected (and some addicted) by what can never satisfy but may succeed in blocking God out of people's minds.

If we seek a Christian mind on abortion or euthanasia, the fact of God will affect our view of 'the right to abortion, the right to die'. Are we in charge of life – or is God? It makes a profound difference. We will start with a view of the sanctity of life and see the tragedy that career convenience or other social reasons can lead to killing. Righteous anger will mingle with aching hearts for those involved.

If we look at advertising, our God-marker will alert us to the exclusively this-worldly nature of the whole industry. In this and countless other areas, we will want both to protest and to plead: 'There is more. You have left the major part of life out of account. You're playing God and you don't know how. Let God be God.'

2. Creation

God made this world and it is his. This establishes both its ownership and its wonder. The Christian sees every aspect of this present order as from God and his designing hand. We will note the effects of the fall in the next section, but the Christian affirms with Paul that 'everything God created is good, and nothing is to be rejected if it is received with thanksgiving, because it is consecrated by the Word of God and prayer' (1 Timothy 4:4–5). Everything is good: crafts, construction, food, art, music, beauty, marriage, relationships, literature, flowers, hills, lakes, the seasons, history, recreation ... the list could go on and on.

A Christian mind sets out with a positive view of life in this world. Everything is to be received and enjoyed. In principle all those spheres and activities are proper for the Christian and it is only false asceticism that denies them. 'God ... richly provides us with everything for our enjoyment', which Paul gives as a reason not to be arrogant or put our hope in wealth (1 Timothy 6:17).

A biblical mind therefore does not tie us down to narrowly spiritual activities, but opens all creation to us. Some Christians are only half-alive to what God is constantly offering. Of course, a Christian will keep a sense of proportion and priorities, but will want to make sure that his or her mind is as whole-creation as God's. This, incidentally, should also make Christians more interesting as people.

This means that Christians can go with a good conscience into a variety of walks of life. Full-time service is not the only spiritual option. God wants to keep all facets of his creation moving and wants his people in all parts of the big machine – from banking to book-binding, from computing to child-raising, from orchestras to ornithology, from historical research to horticulture. And even professional sport?

A Christian will be free, according to his or her interests and time, to go to concerts, read novels, take up crafts, play an instrument, entertain international students or enjoy gardening ... and much more.

This means that Christians will want to carry God's creation mind into all areas of life. They will affirm the biblical view of heterosexuality and marriage (over against homosexual practice). They will affirm the value of work in itself, and not measure people's worth by their salary. They will try to discern what the Bible actually says about the family and put career ambitions in that context.

3. Human rebellion and sin

The fall followed creation. This does not cancel the Christian view of creation, or Paul would not have written what he did. But it does enter a serious caution. What God gave in his goodness as creator now has to be 'consecrated', since it has been tainted and can be distorted by sin. Everything good can be twisted and exploited. We have to be told to be 'generous and willing to share' (1 Timothy 6:18), because our fallen nature is to covet and hoard.

The Christian mind sees the crippling effects of sin and human selfishness affecting every area of creation. Music schools can be places of unholy competitiveness, ambition and bitchiness. Pulpits can be places of outsize egos. Life can be held cheap by the power-hungry. Families can be zones of daily verbal murder. Beautiful sunsets can be spoilt by petty arguments.

The Christian will bring this sad marker to bear on every issue that arises. It will colour his or her attitude to the topics we have touched on – the lottery, abortion and euthanasia and advertising. Advertising has been raised to an art-form, far more entertaining than much entertainment. But a Christian will hardly be at ease with its constant here-and-now focus or with its concentration on the superficial (beauty aids, deodorants, image-enhancers) and on status (the car you drive, the card you use, the holidays you take, the clothes you sport).

Harry Blamires cited a bank's advertisement, which included the question: 'How do your neighbours rate *you*?'

He characterized the advertisement as a crude appeal to vanity and snobbery and commented:

> Suppose I were to ask a few questions. Are there Christians on this bank's Board of Directors? Are they ashamed of themselves? Are they going to do anything about it? If I were to ask these questions ... I should be asked to describe what possible connection there could be between having Christians on the Board and publishing or not publishing the advertisement. If I were to speak christianly about this ... I should find myself treated as an eccentric lost in a private world of fantasy ... Yet, to be honest, I find this advertisement an evil thing (from *The Christian Mind* [SPCK, 1963], p. 30).

Whether or not we sit on Boards that can affect such things, we should certainly have a Christian mind to understand (and when appropriate to point out) the effects of sin distorting God's world and narrowing people's lives and horizons. Or, in the case of abortion and euthanasia, removing people's lives. The Christian mind can never forget an awareness of evil. If a Christian reads a novel or watches a TV drama, one question will be: is this simply revelling in the dirt of the human gutter? Or is some other purpose involved? What values come across? What is this saying about society?

When sin gets a grip and God is no longer in the frame, everything in society gets out of proportion, from judicial systems and scales of punishment to notions of fame or priorities in personal lives. A Christian mind will certainly want to ask in any sphere: how has this been affected by sin?

4. Jesus Christ, the Son of God

On every issue and in every situation the Christian will always want to ask: 'What is Christ's mind on this? What would he say?' This is another way of taking us back to the Bible, for the Father and the Son and the Spirit have one mind, revealed there. But it is helpful to personalize it in relation to the Master, so that we also see that it is not some abstract, impersonal stance, but *his* own view. He sees the world as under God, created and fallen. He wept over stubborn Jerusalem; and sin today is not against a dry code, but against him still.

On many issues Jesus made specific statements – on possessions, riches, joy, happiness, purpose, guilt, destiny. They define sharply the outlines of a Christian mind, but always against the backdrop of the grace he offers. It is easy for a Christian mind in a fallen world to adopt the posture of censure – which is often justified. But it betrays the Lord Jesus if the church's message to the world is just one of moral condemnation and not also one of grace and the offer of forgiveness. He came to seek and to save. He did not have much time for the self-righteous, but plenty for others.

He affirms that the Christian mind always has concern for the person. And when the standard objection to Christianity comes up yet again (How can a God of love allow suffering?), Christ stands there, saying: 'I suffered. I died. I chose to, freely. I was forsaken, though innocent. I know what that was like – *and* I did it for you.' The Christian mind always wants to find appropriate ways to speak of Jesus, also knowing that everything we have that is good comes to us because Jesus made peace for us on the cross.

5. The climax

This marker brings us back to the eternal perspective. This world is temporary, inconclusive in the sense that the conclusion of resurrection and judgment is beyond this sphere of time. 'We brought nothing into the world, and we can take nothing out of it' (1 Timothy 6:7). We are 'destined to die once, and after that to face judgment' (Hebrews 9:27).

So the biblical mind will always ask: how does this issue – lottery, life, advertising, ambition, politics – relate to eternity? What is it doing for people's destiny? How important is it in the light of judgment? Some things do not ultimately matter at all, such as how much we have in our bank. Some things do, and the Christian is concerned to carry and convey the urgency of the coming day, when time will end and opportunity pass for ever.

That 'day of the Lord' enables Christians to have an urgency for others while knowing a contentment for themselves. Life is in the hands of God. His diary is operating the world. In a world that has ceased to fear God and now fears anything, the Christian knows that the fear of the Lord casts out all other fears. He has a mind that can face death and dying and can convey this hope to a dying world.

Why not try out some questions of your own against these markers? Take an issue from your daily paper, or the conversation at work or school and think through: what do these markers have to say about this issue? Or do it with a bunch of Christian friends. You can unpack each marker to whatever depth you like, as you draw out more and more of the implications of God's character or the consequences of creation.

Many more examples could be given. Every kind of

issue can be brought to the grid of these markers. This process will not yield neat answers, but it does put before us some of the key questions. If we follow them through, we will at least begin to know what to think. That in turn will help us to know what (and what not) to defend in the name of Christianity. We will have more of a handle on life's questions and may be able to be coherent when our non-Christian friends ask: 'What do you, as a Christian, think about … ?' An explanation is at least half-way to a defence. And asking the right questions is the key.

Many issues – for example, in the realm of medical ethics – are very complex and need a firm grasp of many facts or views before any answer can be offered. Such a grasp does not come easily or by accident; and sometimes we may not get our 'Christian mind' round the issues as we would like. At such points we will need to keep on reflecting on the Bible and the issues. In some ways, this is a life-time enterprise. At least, however, we can start from the certainty of the markers – the great central facts and truths of the Christian faith.

I was conditioned

At every meal the whole family was present. There was a closing as well as an opening prayer, and a chapter of the Bible was read each time. The Bible was read through from Genesis to Revelation. At breakfast or at dinner, as the case might be, we would hear of the New Testament, or of 'the children of Gad after their families, of Zephon and Haggi and Shuni and Ozni, or Eri and Areli.' I do not claim that I always fully understood the meaning of it all. Yet of the total effect there can be no doubt.

The Bible became for me, in all its parts, in every syllable, the very Word of God. I learned that I must believe the Scripture story, and that 'faith' was a gift of God. What had happened in the past, and particularly what had happened in the past in Palestine, was of the greatest moment to me. In short, I was brought up in what Dr. Joad would call 'topographical and temporal parochialism'. I was 'conditioned' in the most thorough fashion. I could not *help believing* in God – in the God of Christianity – in the God of the whole Bible!

Living next to the Library of Congress, you were not so restricted. Your parents were very much enlightened in their religious views. They read to you from some *Bible of the World* instead of from the Bible of Palestine. No, indeed, you correct me, they did no such thing. They did not want to trouble you about religious matters in your early days. They sought to cultivate the 'open mind' in their children.

Shall we say then that in my early life I was conditioned to believe in God, while you were left free to develop your own judgment as you pleased? But that will hardly do. You know as well as I that every child is conditioned by its environment. You were as thoroughly conditioned *not* to believe in God as I was to believe in God. So let us not call each other names. If you want to say that belief was poured down *my* throat, I shall retort by saying that unbelief was poured down *your* throat. That will get us set for our argument.

Cornelius Van Til in *Why I Believe in God* (The Orthodox Presbyterian Church, USA).

16
Speaking up

'You never really understand a person until you consider things from his point of view – until you climb into his skin and walk round in it.'

So spoke Atticus Finch, the wise old small-town lawyer of Maycomb, Alabama. He was talking to his young daughter when she was angry after a day of misfortunes from other people. He meant it metaphorically. God did it literally – climbing into our skin and walking round in it when his Son became man.

Took human nature

That description, of course, does not begin to do justice to the incarnation. Indeed, by itself it borders on an old heresy, if it be taken to imply that God only 'wore our skin'. God did not merely dress up as a man; he became truly and fully man. He did not merely take on human appearance or adopt a human vantage-point; he took human nature to himself. He was made man.

On a full view of the Word made flesh, however, Atticus's phrase has point: God climbed into our skin and sinlessly walked this earth in it for over thirty years. He died in it, rose in it glorified and in it ascended to heaven. That is the method which God chose to achieve the rescue of his people. By climbing into our situation he was able to lift us out of it.

Brilliant innovation

God's way was brilliantly innovative, effective and straightforward: go where they are, become one of them, sit where they sit, suffer what they suffer, live as they live.

Jesus looked out on others through human eyes. He saw things from their perspective (which does not mean he always approved their viewpoint). His was not a mission to them by an outsider so much as a life among them as an insider. He knew what it felt like to be human, to be hungry and harassed, tired and lonely. He also experienced what it was to be outcast, despised and rejected.

Silent years

What was happening to Jesus all those years through his teens and twenties, those years about which we know virtually nothing? The gospels' silence seems to tell us that it doesn't matter for us to know precisely what he did in those years; sufficient to infer that he was living and moving, relating and working, being private and being sociable, thinking and praying, as a – as *the* – human being. He was where we are. He had climbed in: that was the point.

He did not stand outside the world, prodding it from a distance to do better. He was here, the *man* Christ Jesus.

In this way the Son of God was totally in touch both with God his Father *and* with human beings. He was one with God and one with us.

He knew, he was there

This enabled him to speak and live with unavoidable authority. No-one could ever accuse him of standing on the other side and shouting across to us. No-one could dismiss him by saying: 'You don't know what it is like to be me, in my situation.' He knew. He was in it too, and in it to save us.

The fact that he came to save us, the lost, from judgment is what prompts all true Christian care and compassion. Primarily it compels us to make Christ known through the gospel, but it runs on into concern to show compassion in a needy world. The idea is implicit in the second commandment: to love our neighbours as we love ourselves. Loving myself means seeing life from my angle; loving my neighbour means standing in his or her shoes and seeing things from there. From this stems the great story of Christian care to the poor, the hungry, the helpless, the powerless. William Wilberforce, the prime mover in the abolition of slavery in 1833, stood where the slaves stood. Christians today are standing where AIDS victims or refugees stand. Such concern and involvement are clear consequences of the gospel, as we have seen already.

The pattern

This idea of Christ coming down sets the pattern for how Christ wants us to pass on his message. Paul implies as much in his famous self-description in 1 Corinthians 9:16. He declared: 'I am compelled to preach.' That was the same purpose Jesus claimed: to preach is 'why I have come' (Mark 1:38). Paul tells us how he set about it: 'To the Jews I became like a Jew … I have become all things to all people so that by all possible means I may *save* some' (1 Corinthians 9:19–22).

Paul *became* what they were: that is the thrust of his 'by all possible means'. Had he been living now, he might well have used literature, radio, TV, the world-wide web, and so on, but he meant something far more important – all possible means of climbing into other people's skins and seeing life from there. In that way he too was in touch with God *and* with people. Even an apostle's evangelism would have been ineffective had he not 'become all things'.

No technique or formula

This idea has implications for our evangelism. Often our witness does not make much sense to us (still less to our hearers?). That is sometimes because we reduce it to a technique (the cold drop) or a formula. It begins to make sense when we see that it is essentially a going to people and being among them, identifying with them. It is not a sudden blitz or a brief bombardment; it is taking up residence – 'the Word made his dwelling among *us*' (John 1:14).

Such 'living among' may not reach many people at first; it may concentrate on individuals as Jesus often did. It will certainly mean dealing with people as people, not merely as 'souls'.

Obvious advantages

The wisdom and therefore the advantages of this approach are obvious. We meet people on their ground, in their familiar surroundings, in their homes, in their language, according to their style and ways. We thereby take away many barriers to the gospel until the only one that's left is the offence of Christ himself.

In this approach it is we Christians who have to make the effort, rather than demanding it of others. We have to get up out of our seats and go, rather than expecting them to get out of theirs and come. This makes us put ourselves out, as Jesus put himself out of heaven. This climbing into their skin may make us keep our voices down; you can't 'proclaim the gospel' across a cup of coffee in a preaching, still less a shouting, voice. You have to respect them and their ethos.

Opposite direction

Much of our evangelism goes in the opposite direction, to get them on to our patch, under our church roof. We like it this way, because we can measure our results and keep tabs on what people are doing. God has undoubtedly used these methods, but even as we try to clear the way for people to come, we are erecting extra hurdles for them to jump.

What would we feel like if asked to enter a Christian Science meeting or a Kingdom Hall? Strange, uncertain, slightly threatened? So do many people who are invited to the average evangelical church or event. And all because the direction is from them to us rather than from us to them. The pattern in the Christmas story is 'from him to us and from us to them'.

In touch with people

We may be in touch with God and his message, but we need also to be in touch with people. Do we give the impression to the outsider that we know what it is like to be him or her, that we know the world he inhabits? Do we treat him or her as a gospel target or as a whole person? We make life much harder for the success of the gospel by being so stuck to *buildings, patterns* (even good ones), *meetings* and *services*. God the Father sent his Son into the *world* (John 17:18); we are in it, but seldom going into it as he did. The whole idea seems risky (the incarnation 'idea' cost the son of God his life), whereas the 'them to us' idea is safer and manageable. But which is the right basic direction?

This idea has another advantage. It uses, depends on and dignifies the members of the church. It shows the reason why God has scattered his people through society: personal assistants and plumbers, designers and decorators, home helps and hospital staff, computer programmers and car salesmen, journalists and lawyers, engineers and miners, MPs and sports people, neighbours and friends. Those people – that's us – are those who are out there with people, doing the same jobs, sharing the same lives.

No accident

This is certainly not disparaging those in 'full-time service', if they too are actually 'becoming all things to win some'. But 95% of God's people are 'ordinary members', and that's no accident on God's part. These are the folk who are full-time where other people are, and their life and impact *are* the missionary people-power of the church. We find ourselves in the 'us to them' mode, in the pattern of Jesus himself. Such 'ordinary members' are where others laugh and cry, worry and relax, celebrate and commiserate, work and play. We are with them, provided we have not acquired so much church-cred that we've lost all street-cred. The church should be at its best Monday to Saturday, in the world.

It is from this that opportunities to speak arise or are created. It is when this happens that Christians get involved in caring and helping others. It arises naturally out of their living contact. It is good neighbourliness in action. It shows Christians' love in action and powerfully backs up what they say. It is grassroots Christian concern for others in the totality of their lives – like Jesus.

Being alongside

Moreover, this pattern does not depend on having gifts or being gifted. We don't have to be great evangelists, quick on our feet in debate, able to turn every conversation to the gospel in thirty seconds. We just have to be *us* alongside others, doing our best with the Spirit's help to be *there*, with them, listening, climbing into their skin and walking round. This pattern will use any gift we've got, but is equally possible for those who think they have no special gift.

'Becoming all things' is risky. It got Jesus and Paul roundly criticized, especially by the super-spiritual. It brought temptations into the experience of the Lord. But it was his way. In our churches we need to upgrade the office of 'ordinary member out in the world', helping them to be Christians *there*.

This is the starting-point of the Christian concept of mission and it has two important consequences.

Something to say

The first consequence is that, when we are 'in other people's shoes', alongside them and accepted, we need to have something to say and to be willing to say it. It is little use just being there and being nice and affirming. It is the message, the gospel that is the power of God to save people; faith comes from hearing the word of Christ (Romans 1:16; 10:17). So we need to be able to explain the nature and relevance of Christianity; to defend it against current objections or attacks; to show its coherence; to demonstrate how it ties in with reality; to show how it explains the human condition – and much more. We need to know the truth of Christianity so that we have confidence in the gospel.

I recently had a pleasant little surprise. Some years ago, after regularly getting wet through on climbing holidays in a cheap 'all-weather' jacket, I splashed out on a brand-name storm-proof one. That was fine, until it too gradually ceased to be waterproof. I sent it back for re-proofing, expecting to pay. The reply was: 'We'll replace it free.' I hadn't even asked for a replacement, but they were obviously jealous for their name. Now I sport the latest version of an expensive garment – free. Whenever I wear it, I want to say to others: 'Guess how I got this!' I've been so delighted that I've wanted to talk about it. But I've put on Christ. Why am I not so eager to talk about him?

Now that is not a totally fair analogy and could easily load us with guilt if we left it there. I can expect those I talk to about my jacket immediately to share my delight; there is no down-side for them, nothing that impinges on them (unless they want to send their old one back). Talking about Christ is harder, because there is a down-side to the gospel if they don't accept it and there is a cost if they do.

There is no good news in Christ without at least some

element of the 'bad' news of how God views those who do not repent. 'It is not the healthy who need a doctor, but the sick', as Jesus said (Luke 5:31). So, when we do have some grasp of the gospel, it is a serious question as to how we can begin to engage in conversation about it. How do opportunities to speak of Christ arise? What points of contact are there with postmodern people who seem oblivious to anything 'religious'? Four suggestions may help us to get started.

First, as we have said, we need to be with others; to be a friend, someone who has fun and shares worries, who listens, who is always there, especially when needed. Watch videos with them, have meals together, help each other with DIY jobs. God can give us openings in casual conversations, but basically means us to be in ongoing friendships with others, remembering that friendship can be at different levels. Genuine friendship is quite rare today, so true friendship will be valued.

Bruce Milne makes sense when he says: 'Our failures in evangelism are often failures in love … People want to know that we care before they care about what we know.'

Secondly, we need to be alert for any serious conversation – not solemn, but serious. As we have seen, serious conversation is not very far from a Christian conversation. It may spring up over a film or book, over an item in the day's news, over politics or sport, over a personal tragedy or a broken relationship, over the lyrics of a song or the wording of an advertisement. We need to welcome any serious reflection that arises in the midst of society's trivial pursuits.

At those points we need to know how to explain and apply Christianity. This has been necessary in all generations; it is particularly so today. Christianity faces all kinds of objections that seem to pull the rug from under it even before we start. An age which prizes tolerance above all virtues rejects the thought of Jesus as the only way. A culture that emphasizes everyone's freedom to make up their own values does not welcome the idea of one authoritative revelation from God. A freewheeling society spurns any notion of judgment. Postmodern people see no reason to look at evidence for the resurrection. Many still believe that 'science' has debunked religion or that psychology has explained it away or that it is all the result of sociological factors. As Christians we need to have some answers to such questions.

For help in this area, *Discovering Christianity* by Richard Cunningham (UCCF) is an excellent manual, based on John's Gospel. It covers all the major areas that come up in conversations about faith and it is set out for group or individual use. Or there is James Sire's *The Universe Next Door* (IVP, 1997), a great introduction to the various worldviews and how to discuss them. For a booklet-size explanation of the gospel, *Two Ways to Live* is excellent (Phillip Jensen, St. Matthias Press, 1989).

Thirdly, we can usefully prepare for speaking Christianly by taking time to reflect on and analyse what our non-Christian friends believe. They all have a belief-system, whether they know it or not. They all believe something about themselves, about right and wrong, about happiness, about death, and so on. A little time spent recalling their remarks and reactions may well give us material for future conversations, if only to note that they believe something and to enquire gently as to why they believe it. Maybe a few Christians you know well can think through together what their friends' beliefs are.

Fourthly, we can look for the points where the belief-system of our non-Christian friends lets them down. Many know they struggle to define and discover their own identity or the source of happiness. Many have an acute sense of needing to belong, but know they don't. Many wrestle with insecurity or meaninglessness. Many have no idea how to come to good ethical decisions. All such topics are potential starting-points for serious and Christian conversation. It does not matter too much what we start talking about, since all truth is God's truth and eventually will connect to Christ.

Covers the world

The other consequence of this view of Christian mission is that it covers the world. The 'in their shoes' model is the basis of world mission and has led countless thousands of Christians down the centuries to immerse themselves in other people's cultures so that they can talk of Christ as insiders to insiders. Such lifestyles are costly, as the many Christian martyrs testify (more in our century, it is claimed, than in all previous ones put together). Why have Christians like us been willing to put their lives at risk of ill-health, poverty, loneliness and early death? Because they believed as fact that this world is lost without Christ. Without him people are going to hell. 'They will go away to eternal [everlasting] punishment, but the righteous to eternal [everlasting] life' (Matthew 25:46). One destiny or the other. If it is the former, 'the smoke of their torment rises for ever and ever' (Revelation 14:11). All roads do not lead to God. We have to ask ourselves if we seriously believe this.

This is why Christ said: 'Ask the Lord of the harvest, therefore, to send out workers into his harvest field' (Matthew 9:38). The harvest refers to the end of the age, to the day of judgment; it is because that day is coming that workers are needed to alert people now to their destiny. That is Jesus' own verdict; people need to hear. He does not assume that they will come to him unconsciously or without hearing. The field will not grow indefinitely; the day of harvest will come, irreversibly.

New methods

Certainly there are many methods of spreading the gospel now that did not exist for the early church, or the medieval church, or even the twentieth-century church, twenty years ago. Closed countries are now being penetrated by truth on the world-wide web; censorships are being bypassed by the same means. But God still wants people to get alongside people. We can do this in full-time Christian service or in jobs and professions, each according to God's way for us.

If we are moved by Christ's coming into our world and into our shoes; if we are saved by this one, sufficient sacrifice on the cross; if we have our eyes and hopes on heaven and the real world to come; then we are already caught up in his saving purpose. That purpose is and was for the world. The only question is how and where we show our involvement. To live for that purpose is the only course that honours God and makes sense of life.

Conclusion:
Looking forward

From the Bible we *can* see sense in our lives; so where do we go from here? Getting God's perspective on our Christian life will have a huge impact on any life. It will satisfy us intellectually, stimulate us spiritually, uplift us emotionally, and transform our lives.

We looked at Peter's message and his method in Chapter 3. In his second letter we saw that his method was clear: first, understand; second, respond. In that order. This book has tried to outline the Bible's understanding of the ways of God and of our Christian lives; now, what response is appropriate?

Peter's method was essentially to work from what they knew about the end of the age to how they should live now: 'Since everything will be destroyed in this way, what kind of people ought you to be? You ought to live holy and godly lives as you look forward to the day of God and speed its coming' (2 Peter 3:11–12). 'We are looking

forward', he repeats; and again, 'since you are looking forward ... make every effort to be found spotless, blameless
and at peace with him' (2 Peter 3:13–14). 'Therefore ...
since you already know this, be on your guard ...' (2 Peter
3:17).

Peter's method is the Bible's method and gives us our
lead. First the truth, then the consequences. First the
understanding, then the practice. First the picture, then
the imperative. Since everything is as God has shown us,
since the Bible throws light on our life and gives sense to
our experiences, we ought to respond by godly lives that
are at peace with him.

Peter uses absolute terms (spotless, blameless), not
because he thinks we can attain perfection here, but
because he is looking for an absolute commitment to God
and his cause. No half-measures. No limp response. No
divided heart. No playing games with God. No delaying
tactics.

On the basis of the sense God has made of our lives, by
the once-for-all revelation in his Word and the once-for-all
atonement of his Son, we cannot do less than give ourselves to 'grow in the grace and knowledge of our Lord and
Saviour Jesus Christ' and to make sure our lives give glory
to him (2 Peter 3:18).

God wants changed perspectives to make changed
people who will make a difference in this world for him.
Why not us? Starting now, starting here – and ending in
glory.